TURNING TOWARD HAPPINESS

Conversations with a Zen Teacher and Her Students

Edited by Sara Jenkins

PRESENT PERFECT BOOKS

The Blessed One, knowing of the mental agitations

going on in the minds of those assembled, . . .

his great heart moved by compassion, smiled and said:

In the days of old . . . fully enlightened Ones

came to the Castle of Lanka on Mount Malaya

and discoursed on the Truth of Noble Wisdom

that is beyond the reasoning knowledge of the philosophers . . .

and which is realizable only within the inmost consciousness;

for your sakes, I too would discourse on the same Truth.

The Lankavatara Scripture

CONTENTS

INTRODUCTION

The Center for the Practice of Zen Buddhist Meditation occupies a small frame house on a corner in a town south of San Francisco. Half-hidden under the dense foliage of a loquat tree, it offers no information identifying it as a Zen Center. Once you pass through the picket fence, though, you can see onto the porch where certain telltale signs suggest what goes on inside. Under a bench are one or two or ten or fifteen pairs of shoes. Above, a bulletin board is feathered with schedules for guidance appointments, sign-up sheets for retreats, and cartoons about meditation and enlightenment.

Through the doorway you can glimpse a row of black meditation cushions along a wall. The building is open daily and houses the administrative office, but many Center activities also take place elsewhere in the Bay Area. A weekly sitting and discussion group meets in San Francisco, and workshops are held at various locations. Regular retreats, lasting from a weekend to thirty days, are offered at the Center's monastery in the Sierra foothills. Twice a year, ten-day retreats are held at a Catholic convent in Carmel.

The teacher at the Center is named Cheri. I first met her at a time when I believed that I needed to do something about my life, and Zen Buddhist meditation seemed suitably drastic. On the other hand, I was reluctant to undertake a spiritual path that I associated with cumbersome robes, submissive behavior, and foreign terminology, not to mention a certain machismo. I also suspected that Zen — no matter how simply or earnestly or entertainingly presented — would always elude me. Then, too, affiliation with a Zen Center might be uncomfortable to explain in my professional life; I could imagine this information as an eccentric note in an otherwise respectable biographical sketch. But when a friend urged me attend a discussion Cheri was leading, desperation won out over resistance, hopelessness, and apprehension.

That first time I heard Cheri speak, I figured my comprehension level to be around five percent. And yet much was communicated. Her desire to share the truth of this path — her willingness to repeat, to elaborate, to patiently try another and yet another way to make it clear — suggested a momentousness to what she had to say, even some urgency. At the same time, her humor demonstrated a lightness of spirit, insisted that things might be all right after all. (Now that's an authentic Zen laugh, I remember thinking.) There was something about her that I experienced as wide-openness, terrifying yet irresistible; something I saw as freedom; something I felt as love — and all that made me think that the most important thing in my life was to hear more.

When I try to say what I have learned during the five years I have been listening to Cheri, one word always comes to mind: happiness. When I try to describe the practice that she teaches, it is always with two words: ending suffering. In

Buddhism, ordinary life is likened to the turning of a wheel, in which suffering is the inevitable consequence of actions that arise in ignorance of our true nature. The path taught by the Buddha enables us to stop that wheel and turn it in the other direction, toward happiness. If the word happiness is rarely encountered in most Buddhist teaching, that is because striving to attain happiness is at best only temporarily successful. Instead, this path aims specifically at ending suffering: once we end our suffering, happiness is what is there. How to do that — how to turn the wheel in the opposite direction — is the subject of this book.

But if the path of Zen is as fundamentally experiential as it is said to be, what use is language? Much more time is spent in silent meditation than listening to the teacher. Furthermore, Zen teachers are renowned for speaking in a highly cryptic manner. And even when a student suddenly understands — whether in listening to a talk or directly interacting with the teacher — it is difficult to answer the question, understands what?

On the other hand, language has played an important role in my experience of this practice. Those verbal expressions that initially leave me most baffled are the ones that stick with me no matter how I resist and deny and try to ignore them. The very words used to describe the most mystifying and paradoxical concepts seem to sink into the depths of awareness and lie dormant until conditions are right for them to pop to the surface — where, I have found again and again, they suddenly and perfectly illuminate a situation I had been blind to. Even those maddeningly pointless little Zen tales: I admit that some of them have unexpectedly enabled me to make sense of certain experiences, and I have faith that others are still lurking, waiting for their moment. So, if parts of this book seem puzzling, even troubling, it is my hope that they will settle into someone's heart, to grow and coalesce and finally to unfurl as new understanding: "Ah, *this* is what that

11

meant . . . ." I also hope that some ineffable quality of Cheri's presence might infuse these pages, for that is the breath of liberation that has made the words live for me.

—

As a way of offering a framework for approaching these discussions (and this practice) — in which there is no beginning and no end, no logical progression — I herewith summarize what I think of as Essential Buddhism.

The Buddha (it is said), even when asked, refrained from addressing questions of the relation of body and soul, whether the universe is infinite and eternal, how we got here, and what happens after we die. The Buddhist path has a single purpose: to end suffering. "Suffering" here does not mean physical pain or grief or anger or any unpleasant experiences in themselves. We may or may not suffer with a given experience, and that may change from one time to another. Suffering means our *reaction* to not getting our way and may range from trivial irritation to violent destructiveness. When meditation students discuss their struggles with such inconveniences as traffic jams and long lines at the bank, they do not mean to suggest that these constitute such unbearable suffering that they were driven to the likes of Zen. The process at the heart of this path is to watch everything: much is learned by observing the simplest instances of our wanting things to be other than they are.

We think we will get what we want by struggling against what we don't like. But this assumes that we are separate from the world; otherwise there would be nothing to struggle against. This misconception arises as part of our socialization: in developing our identities as individuals, we learn to maintain a sense of separateness from everything else. Although this conditioning is unavoidable, suffering is not: the Buddhist path, described in innumerable ways through two millennia and many cultures, offers a method for ending our suffering. (Not that Cheri puts much emphasis on what the

Buddha may have said. She recommends that if you want to read about spiritual practice, that's fine, but spend as much time in sitting meditation as you do in reading — and always sit first.)

Zen is one version of this path. It is a spiritual practice that does not include religious beliefs. Zen might be likened instead to an experimental study in which the laboratory is the whole of our experience. We scrutinize the same phenomena over and over again, we raise question after question, trying to uncover the source of our dissatisfaction. Eventually, we see exactly how suffering arises as we turn away from our hearts, from our own innate goodness and sufficiency. We also observe how suffering loosens its grip on us once we see into the nature of our conditioning.

Here are some things I have learned through this practice that each of us can experience for ourselves:

- No matter what, we can always find refuge in the present moment.
- When suffering continues to arise, we can always meet it with compassion.
- Compassion for ourselves automatically results in compassion for everything.
- We are absolutely responsible for our own experience.

Only when we abandon ourselves in the illusion that the world requires something more of us than we are — the illusion that we are separate from the world — do we lack anything. When we are fully present to ourselves, we can rest secure that we are doing our best to care for that aspect of the world for which we alone are responsible, ourselves: when we are hungry, we will eat; if we are lonely, we will provide our own best company. Simply by being with ourselves, we have everything we need.

What does it mean to "be with oneself"? Various techniques can help us know that experience in different ways. Accepting the precepts (given in the next section) as guidelines for our lives brings all our actions under scrutiny and thus aids in ending our suffering. Learning to identify aspects of the conditioned self as subpersonalities* can be helpful in developing the habit of observing one's inner states rather than becoming absorbed in them. And an awareness of subpersonalities makes it easier to see the process of projection, or how we experience the world through the conditioned responses arising from our sense of separateness. To assert that our view of the world is projected from within ourselves flies in the face of "common sense" and fundamental assumptions about causality. But to investigate this possibility with an open mind is to begin to discover how we operate in ways that cause us to suffer. Once we see how projection works, we can be released from the pattern of blame and guilt that poisons our relationships and move into the freedom of accepting full responsibility for our lives.

Sitting in meditation is the central technique in this path of inquiry, the best opportunity to be present to oneself. The purpose of Zen meditation is not to cultivate calmness or deep concentration, nor to find answers, much less the magically enduring bliss most of us hope for. When we sit in meditation, our minds wander, and the way in which we return our attention to the present provides an instant display of how we deal with ourselves — and how we are with ourselves is how we are in the world. In observing with full acceptance whatever distracts us, and gently returning the attention to the present, we discover both what prevents us from enjoying the sufficiency of the moment and how to let go of that resistance to whatever is happening. It is possible to see, for example,

---

*The concept of subpersonalities comes from a method of self-realization described by Roberto Assagioli (*Psychosynthesis*, 1971, Penguin) and is used in other meditation groups as well. Although it sounds like modern psychology, the same idea seems to appear in an ancient Buddhist text, The Sutra of Hui-neng, where students are urged to become acquainted with "the sentient beings within our mind," which are described as "the delusive mind, the deceitful mind, the evil mind, and such like . . . ."

after long struggle, that struggle itself is the problem. Sitting offers an opportunity to be with ourselves, through the struggle, in kindness and acceptance and gentleness, to establish the habit of willingness to experience anything that arises. In moments when the resistance ceases, we see its utterly superfluous nature, and we exist in perfect ease. And even a single moment of freedom from suffering — just sitting there *without* struggling — is enough to know that freedom is possible for everybody. In such moments of freedom, we find that hatred, conflict, greed simply are not there. Change is there, always; but not suffering.

This Zen teacher named Cheri never misses an opportunity to remind us that, as she likes to put it, *suffering is not a requirement.* (The Zen Center even has T-shirts with words to that effect.)

For me, this unlikely idea has often been demonstrated wordlessly in individual guidance appointments. The first time I sat opposite Cheri, I discovered that I had nothing to say, because suddenly, as we simply sat there on our black cushions, nothing was wrong. Other encounters have had enough of the legendary fearsomeness of traditional Zen teacher-student interactions for me to be convinced that this is nevertheless the real thing; in such sessions, the bruising my ego takes is a measure of my attachment to the issue at hand.

Mostly, though, the image of guidance appointments that arises in my mind is two chairs set outside, facing a stream or a grassy hillside or a flowering tree or the ocean, or set in the sunny side yard of the Zen Center house, in full view of everyone but just out of earshot, the chairs turned slightly toward each other, and the two of us laughing together at the endless ploys of egocentricity and the non-necessity of taking it all too seriously.

—

My interest here is to show something of the process of teaching and learning at this particular Zen Center: how the practice is presented by this teacher, how it is assimilated and articulated by students, how it is shared within the group. In matters of the spirit, it seems, what strikes one person with a profound insight may leave another perplexed. I hope that in these discussions of struggle and acceptance, confusion and understanding, suffering and glimpses of liberation, spoken in this medley of voices — teacher, students, monks — some expression of truth will ring clear. As one of those students, I offer this in gratitude for the guidance I have received, hoping to encourage others on the path that leads to finding refuge within oneself.

❂

THE PRECEPTS

"Taking the precepts" refers to a ceremony in which Zen students publicly accept certain vows. Buddhism includes many precepts, and those administered on a given occasion vary with different traditions. The precepts ceremony performed at this Zen Center includes the Ten Grave Prohibitive Precepts, given in the chart that follows, along with the Three Pure Precepts:

The precept of restraint and religious observances.
This is the practice of restraining oneself, never anyone or anything else. One's work is always with oneself.

The precept of obedience to all good laws.
We don't decide for others. We only perfect ourselves so that we can be ready to share with and guide others.

The precept to benefit all sentient beings.
Compassion toward every being is practiced in thought, word, and deed to the degree that one is capable.

The precepts ceremony neither entitles nor restricts those who make the vows. At the Zen Center and at the monastery, the precepts are recited by everyone each morning before meditation as part of the Daily Recollection. A useful approach to the precepts is suggested in the following statement, taken from the Zen Center's booklet called "In Our Practice":

> We have no creed, no dogma which must be believed and to which one must adhere. Nothing is forbidden. The precepts of this Path are agreements that one makes with oneself, voluntarily, and which one renews each day. We are ever mindful that our commitment is with ourselves and that this is the commitment: "In this way I do most deeply vow to train myself." No one can practice for someone else, and faith that rests on another's authority is not true faith.

Working with the precepts in this way both demands and nourishes the practice of vigilance, openness, and compassion. It is very different from following rules, and this difference is hard for many of us to grasp. In the third part of this book, under "Living the Precepts," the challenges and the rewards of taking these vows are discussed at some length.

The chart of the precepts that follows was developed by a student. In trying to write about the precepts, he had been frustrated by results that sounded like either an intellectual essay or a reform pamphlet, so began experimenting with listing words, phrases, and ideas that came to mind, using the impasses that arose as a sign to turn to inner examination. In the chart form that emerged, the first column contains the literal text of each precept as given in the Daily Recollection. The second gives key terms summing up the meaning of each precept as a virtue. In the third column, the precepts are put in the form of prohibitions. The fourth describes life lived in accordance with each precept. In the last column, fundamental insights (which we may glimpse and then forget) are offered as encouragement to sustain precept practice through times of doubt.

The chart is reprinted from *In Process: A Journal of Spiritual Practice* (February 1991), a collection of anonymous contributions published periodically by the Zen Center.

Precept	Key	Prohibition
Not to lead a harmful life nor to encourage others to do so	Gratitude	Not killing
Not to take that which is not given	Generosity	Not stealing
Not to commit or participate in unchaste conduct	Love	Not lusting
Not to tell lies nor practice believing the fantasies of authority	Honesty	Not lying
Not to use intoxicating drinks or narcotics nor assist others to do so	Awareness	Not clouding
Not to publish other people's faults	Kindness	Not blaming or criticizing
Not to extol oneself and slander others	Humility	Not competing or coveting
Not to be avaricious in bestowal of the teachings	Piety	Not apostatizing or denying spiritual responsibility
Not to be angry	Acceptance	Not to rage, resent, or revenge
Not to speak ill of this religion or any other	Tolerance	Not persecuting or assuming spiritual authority

Aspiration	Inspiration
To live in harmony with all life and the environment which sustains it	There is no separate self
To freely give, ask for, and accept what is needed	There is no scarcity of resources
To give and accept affection and friendship without clinging	There is no scarcity of love
To see and act in accordance with what is	There is no need to hide the truth
To embrace all experience directly	There is no need to hide from the truth
To acknowledge responsibility for everything in my life	There are no victims or perpetrators
To give my best effort and accept the results	There are no winners or losers
To live an openly spiritual life	There is nothing in my life which is not part of my spiritual training
To see everything as an opportunity	There are no mistakes
To encourage others to lead a spiritual life, *in their own way*	There is nothing in anyone else's life which is not appropriate to their spiritual training

ALL THE AWAKENING
WE WOULD EVER DESIRE:
THE TEACHER

Cheri, the teacher at the Zen Center, describes herself simply
as a "guide." Instead of delivering formal talks, she fields
questions, and her responses continually turn us back to
ourselves. In this, her approach to teaching is like that of the
17th century Zen master Bankei. When a student suggested
that he include classic texts and stories of Buddhism in his
talks, Bankei replied:

> I never cite the Buddha's words or the words of Zen
> patriarchs when I teach. All I do is comment directly on
> people themselves. That takes care of everything .... So you
> won't find me saying anything about either the "Buddha
> Dharma" or the "Zen Dharma." I don't have to, when I can
> clear everything up for you by commenting directly on you
> and your personal concerns right here and now.

At the Zen Center the discussions usually begin, in the profound stillness after meditation, with Cheri's question, hardly more than a whisper but perfectly audible throughout the room: "What would you like to talk about?" Someone may describe a problem with sitting practice or a difficult personal situation. Whatever the particular instance of suffering, Cheri makes it clear that we are all in it together. And when she laughs her wonderful laugh, and we find ourselves laughing too, we recognize that there is no need to make things worse by agonizing about them. Then there may come that precious moment when letting go seems possible, and an end to suffering is in sight.

At such moments I remember, once again, that the point is not to suppress the emotions we associate with suffering but to experience them fully, to embrace and observe them and get to know them and simply allow them their existence. Anger, for example, may be experienced in the body as strong sensations of heat and tension; sadness as pressure or weight. These and other feelings come and go like the weather, their causes far too complex for us to unravel, and any illusion of controlling them pure folly. We do better to greet them as we do the changes in clouds, wind, rain. Cheri encourages us to meet all such changes with the same acceptance: "Ah — anger. Ah — rain." Here it is: not a problem.

✦

The Ease and the Difficulty in Letting Go

You certainly must cherish your illusions dearly, for you to change the Buddha-mind into them just so you can be deluded. If you only knew the great value of the Buddha-mind, there's no way you could ever by deluded again . . . . When you are not deluded, you are a Buddha, and that means you are enlightened. There is no other way for you to become a Buddha. So draw close and listen carefully and be sure that you understand what I say.

Zen Master Bankei

Q: How can we tell what is the right thing to do in the moment?

A: For me, the right thing is always to drop everything and come back to the breath. But this is a practice of ending suffering, not of doing the right thing. So as long as we're suffering, we can know — that we haven't ended our suffering. [Laughter]

That's not to say that because we haven't ended our suffering, we must be doing something wrong. It just means we haven't ended our suffering. And listen, this is also true: as long as we *want* to end our suffering, we're going to suffer. I realize that it's this kind of statement that makes it so easy to have a love-hate relationship with Zen.

But in response to the question, it seems to me that all we can do is throw ourselves wholeheartedly into whatever we're doing. With the understanding that we'll do the best we can to keep bringing our attention back to the present and look carefully at whatever is going on. Then if the action we take seems to lead away from suffering, we can know just that: in this moment, in this situation, this action is leading away from suffering.

There's a danger in deciding that whatever you're doing is the "right" thing to do, because action that may lead away from suffering in this situation could plunge you right into suffering in the next one. So we're left once again with the requirement that whatever is going on, we come to the present moment, we pay careful attention. If we are present in the moment, if we're centered and listening to our hearts, we'll be in a good position to make choices that lead toward ending suffering.

How will we know when we're in that position? Well, we can't say exactly. You just sort of know. For one thing, you may notice that you're not suffering.

With each moment, looking at our conditioning, looking at what we cling to, what we resist, what we think, what we believe — we can see all the things we do that cause us to suffer. And each moment we have the opportunity to drop all of that, come back to the breath, come back to our center, to be present.

There's a tendency to idealize awakening, to think that once we awaken, everything will be okay; all the lights will be on, suffering will be ended, and that's that. It would be really regrettable to spend our lives living for that moment — because it isn't like that.

Suzuki-roshi talked about the love of the process of awakening, rather than idealizing a point out there in the future where something is going to happen. Once you love the *practice* of awakening, it won't matter to you whether something called "awakening" ever happens. The moment you love the process of ending suffering, it doesn't matter whether or not suffering ever ends. *That love of the practice of ending suffering will probably be all of the awakening that you would ever desire.* It would be so far beyond your wildest dreams of what life could be like that it would be difficult to imagine anything more wonderful.

Awakening is not getting to a place, it's not accomplishing something, it's not changing anything — it's just learning to love what you do in this moment. It's so much easier than people think. All the other stuff people try to do in spiritual practice makes it much harder than it needs to be. If you could just love the practice, without having standards about what practice should be or how well you're doing it. If you could just love sitting, without having to decide whether it's a good meditation or a bad meditation and comparing it to the one you had last week or reading something in a book about somebody's meditation and thinking you'll never have a meditation like that — if you could just love *sitting* . . . .

Somebody said to me last week, "But I don't know how to do that. It sounds like you're saying to just love, and I can't just love at will." But I think we can. Whenever we are listening to our hearts, love is there. Love is what's there when we stop doing everything else.

Q: Then why don't we just practice that? Is it necessary to really understand so much about the conditioning? A lot of spiritual practices just aim for connecting with that experience of love. They don't look at the conditioning to the extent that we do.

A: Yes, of course, we are attempting to drop our conditioning and get back to our true nature. But people won't do it just like that. It would be wonderful if we could simply drop it. Most of you have had the experience of just dropping it, in the moment. Right? But then it begins to arise again. That's what it comes down to. It's fine for a handful of people who are so karmically primed that they just say, "Sitting in meditation and dropping away mind and body? Yes, that's for me. Where's the cushion?"

But most people go kicking and screaming — to whatever degree they go at all — because the conditioning is so very deep. And that's okay; what we're doing is reversing that process. But we need to realize that usually it happens gradually. So, all this looking at our conditioning is something to do while we build up the courage to just drop it.

Q: We can't just let go, can we? Don't we have to look at what we're letting go of?

A: We *can* just let go, but we don't want to. We like to examine it all first. It's like this yard sale we're having. You could just take home a big box and throw in all the stuff you want to get rid of and deliver it to the Zen Center. But that's not how we do it. We go to the closet and contemplate each item. Before we let go of these treasures, we want to look them over and ponder: What are the chances that this will come back into style? . . . I think I'll just try it on one more time . . . I'd hate to have to buy another one.

Attached as we are to our physical possessions, we are even more attached to our egocentricity. We like to look at all our conditioning over and over and over. In fact, there are people I've worked with for years whose routines I know so well that if they ever were unable to go on, I could go on for them. But we can be considering this same old routine together, and if I suggest simply dropping it, there's usually a lot of resistance.

So — whenever possible, cease to examine, accept everything, get back to the present, let it all go.

And remember to be kind to yourself when it all comes up again.

❁

When You Let Go, You Fall Up

The mind is by nature pure, so there is nothing for us to crave for or give up. Do your best, each of you, and go wherever circumstances lead.

Sixth Zen Patriarch Hui-neng

Q: Doesn't letting go your sense of who you are open a door to greater suffering in some ways?

A: There does seem to be a door there, but when you let go, the suffering is all over. All of this suffering stuff exists only on this side, before you let go. You feel it's going to be awful, you're going to lose everything, you're going to die — and then you let go, and on the other side, what is the experience? None of that was true, was it? In fact, it's wonderful! You wonder what on earth you were doing before, you have this feeling that you were demented. And you were. That's the condition known in Buddhism as "ignorance."

The way this works in terms of emotions is that we keep that door closed to protect ourselves. The door is labeled fear and protection and defense. We keep it closed because we think there's something awful on the other side. But the only problem is that the door is closed. Once we find the willingness to go beyond the fear, to open the door, the whole thing disappears. Door, suffering, the whole nightmare.

There's a critical point in spiritual training, when we recognize all the signs of holding on, all those inner voices, and we know that no matter how convincing those voices are and how loud and desperate and insistent, they are the voices of egocentricity. The voices of suffering. So we just take a deep breath and jump off whatever cliff is in front of us.

And when we fall, we fall up — because there never was any danger, there never was anything to lose. The fear of loss and deprivation is the experience of egocentricity.

So, when you get ready to jump, jump over whatever's there — don't wait for the right thing, just jump.

The suffering is over as soon as you let go.

❂

There Is Nothing Wrong

. . . As it is, whole and complete,
This sense world is enlightenment.

Third Zen Patriarch Seng Tsan

Q: Are there right reasons and wrong reasons for doing things?

A: There are three responses I want to make. One is that there's nothing wrong, and the second is about making mistakes, and the third one — well, I'm sure it will come back to me.

I'm chuckling because many of you must have noticed that I have a standard set of cliches, like, "there's nothing wrong," and what I do up here is just string them together in different ways. But I think these same things are still worth saying because — well, we're all still here. If all of you leave, I'll just continue to say these things to myself, because I'll be the one who still needs to hear them.

So — first, the assumption that something is wrong. When we experience ourselves as separate from everything, there is something wrong, which is that we're not always getting what we want. That's what it comes down to. If we didn't have that ability to experience ourselves as separate, there wouldn't be that problem, because there wouldn't be any way to make comparisons. We wouldn't have a better idea about how things should be — there would just be everything that is. But this subject-object relationship we create causes us to see ourselves as separate and then to decide that there's right and wrong, the world of opposites, and this is where we live.

Second is the idea that I can make a mistake, which is based on the fear of doing something wrong. The path we practice here, the path the Buddha taught, is very different from paths of punishment and reward. Trying to do things right in order to avoid suffering misses the point completely.

That approach is going to get us into trouble immediately.

Ah, here's the third point: I don't happen to believe that there's anything wrong with being in trouble. As far as I can tell, if we want to be free, we have to know how things work. Each moment is my best opportunity to see how I cause myself to suffer: what I'm believing, what I'm clinging to, what I'm pushing away that causes me to suffer. So when something arises, if I cling to it or push it away and then I suffer, I get to see how that happens. And that can be a step toward freedom. Or, when something arises and there's simply being at one with it in that moment, then there's freedom right there. So, just drop it all and get back to the present moment, then there's no problem.

There is nothing wrong. It's not possible to lose. If you make a mistake, you'll learn something. If you don't make a mistake, you'll learn something. If you really want to end suffering, then get right to the present moment and make mistakes just as hard and fast as you can. Find out all the ways you cause yourself to suffer, find the willingness to let go of them, find the compassion for yourself as you go through it all — that's the best you can do.

❂

Bringing Daily Life Into Spiritual Practice

If we are treading the Path of Enlightenment
We need not be worried by stumbling blocks.
Provided we keep a constant eye on our own faults
We cannot go astray from the right path.

Sixth Zen Patriarch Hui-neng

Q: I've been at the monastery for a while, and coming back here, to civilization, I've noticed how often I have to remind myself to bring my attention back to the breath. It's much harder to do that here than it is at the monastery. How do you find the willingness to do the practice in the same way here? Against what feels like overwhelming forces pulling you in the other direction, all those other things that seem so important?

A: We were talking about that the last day of the retreat — not taking spiritual practice into daily life, but bringing daily life into spiritual practice. Accepting the practice as a refuge, as true home. I can go through the day doing whatever I do, with whatever degree of mindfulness, and then there's a feeling of coming home to sitting, to that quiet and comfort and peace. Seeing sitting as that safe place, and bringing all the difficulty — the pain, the disappointment, the frustrations, and so on — into that safe place, so that all that can be healed.

So for those of us who've been away on retreat, it's good as we return to this style of living to remember the vow we take to benefit all beings. That vow leads us to want to embrace the suffering we encounter, here or wherever. Instead of returning to daily life with the feeling that it's going to harm us or hinder us, we can bring it all in to that comfort and safety and security we find at the center of our practice. We can bring the confusion and struggle and anxiety there to be embraced and healed and let go.

It's no good to be afraid of daily life. Nothing's going to happen to you. Nothing's going to happen that hasn't happened already. When we get tired enough of the suffering and beating our heads against the same wall, then we'll remember that we know how to stop it. Everybody in this room knows how to stop, sit down, come back to the breath, and find that stillness. We all know how to do that. If we don't want to, that's different. When it's the most pressing thing in our lives, we'll do it. Until then, there's nothing to fear. And even then, there's nothing to fear! Now or then.

So, being in the world is just a reminder of how nice spiritual practice is. It makes me appreciate this practice. It makes me deeply grateful that there is this practice, and that I know about it and I can do it.

✦

Buddhism

By oneself is evil done; by oneself one is injured. Do not do evil, and suffering will not come. Everyone has the choice to be pure or impure. No one can purify another.

The Dhammapada

Q: Can we really ease someone else's suffering? Isn't the only suffering we can ease our own?

A: We can ease someone else's suffering, in that we can be with one another in ways that are more helpful, more gentle, more kind. But can we take someone's suffering away? Not at all. Although there are ways to contribute to a person's interest in ending their own suffering.

Let me explain how that can work in Buddhism. It's interesting that Buddhism should have survived all this time. There's not a lot of power in it, there's not a lot of money, there's not the stuff we think of as being necessary for survival. Buddhism has always been a religion of demonstration. One person does it, another person sees it and is attracted to it and wants to do it, and so on. There's no proselytizing, no argument for it. There's no idea that you're good if you do it, you're bad if you don't; there's no reward attached. Buddhism doesn't have any of that. It's simply somebody being attracted to the living demonstration of the practice. So in that sense, by being that living expression of the spiritual path, we can ease other people's suffering. My teacher calls it being a "social relief." People don't have to worry about you. They don't have to take care of you, they don't have to be defended against you or be sensitive to you or concerned about upsetting you.

Q: Can you cause anyone else to suffer?

A: No. There is a crucial movement from the idea that "I experience what I experience because things happen to me" to "I experience what I experience because of who I am." That is a night-and-day turn. Until we get to that point, it looks like other people cause our suffering. But in this practice, our purpose is to find out who we are — and then we see where the suffering comes from.

❂

Taking the Precepts

These teachings are only a finger pointing toward Noble Wisdom . . . . They are intended for the consideration and guidance of the discriminating minds of all people, but they are not the Truth itself, which can only be self-realized within one's deepest consciousness.

The Lankavatara Scripture

Q: What does it mean to take the precepts?

A: Does taking precepts necessarily mean anything different from what we're doing now? The answer that occurs to me is that it's like the difference between living together and getting married: it may change something, it may not. If there is a change, it may be for the better, it may be for the worse.

Q: If you look at the statistics on marriage and people who live together, that's not a very good prognosis, is it?

A: That's why I say that. Because often people are willing to do something if there's no commitment, but as soon as there's commitment, all their resistance comes up. In spiritual practice, that's not necessarily a bad thing—it's a big part of what we do spiritual training for. But it's helpful to be prepared for that.

One of the things I like best about Buddhism is that the precepts are simply guidelines. There's no reason you should do them, and nothing's going to happen if you don't do them. If you follow them, that doesn't mean you're a good person; if you don't follow them, that doesn't mean you're a bad person. There isn't any reward for following them, there isn't any punishment for not following them. What the Buddha taught was, if you want to end suffering, here are a few areas it would be helpful to explore, because it is unlikely that you are going to be able or willing to end your suffering as long as you are living a harmful life. It just seems to work that way.

That's all there is to it. So if you want to awaken, it would probably help to try to lead a harmless life.

Now, can you hear that without a "should"? There isn't a "should" in it. It's as simple as this: the odds are that you won't allow yourself to feel good — to be all right with yourself, to be happy — until you are doing what you consider to be good.

So, taking the precepts is just stating an intention. It's an agreement with oneself to do a spiritual practice. It's like deciding on a relationship. Once you make that decision, every time you look at the other person and don't like them, you don't just immediately think you'll get rid of them.

It's like getting to what I call the toothbrushing level of spiritual training. Most of us do not get up in the morning and have a big debate with ourselves about whether we're going to brush our teeth. It's just understood. Even if we're tired, if we don't really feel like it, we still brush our teeth. It's just a part of living. When our spiritual practice moves into that realm, things become easy. But as long as we have debates with ourselves about doing it, it's hard. Because a great deal of that, I would project, is based upon thinking I'm a good person if I do it and I'm not a good person if I don't, and there's a big battle over which is true. But when that decision has been made, when it's simply something I do and I know that I will always do it, then there's a certain relaxation that can happen. For me, that is the beginning of spiritual practice, because then I can settle down to just doing it.

✺

Going the Wrong Way

If there's a trace of right and wrong,
True-mind is lost, confused, distraught.

Third Zen Patriarch Seng Tsan

Q: For those of us who weren't there, could you tell us a little about the precepts ceremony? Rumor has it that there's a great story about somebody going the wrong way. . .

A: Going the wrong way, yes. Some of you know that I am notorious for getting lost. And it's not just too much meditation, it's an actual something in the brain that's not there in me: the sense of direction. I've lived here for six years and I cannot go across town without coming back here first. If I'm at the grocery store and I want to go to the Post Office, I have to come here, not that it's on the way — it's not — but because I don't know how to get there any other way. This is something I've had to make my peace with.

At the precepts ceremony, I went the wrong way. With everybody following me. Only one way existed in my mind; there was no hesitation. I headed out, and all the people taking the precepts were walking with me. And as I was walking along, there was a growing intuition that things didn't look quite right. But then there was sort of a feeling of, "Nah — don't worry," because here at the retreat center where I know where everything is, it just wouldn't be possible to get lost, to go the wrong way.

Eventually, I got to the critical point where I realized I was in the wrong place. So I just turned around and went back. The other people who were involved in the ceremony — I don't want to tell you too much because some of you are going to participate in this ceremony later and I think it's fun not to know how it goes. Anyway, there's stuff that happens that people participating in the ceremony would not ordinarily know about, and it kind of ruins it to know. And when you make an unexpected U-turn and go back, it's all revealed. Like the curtain going up on the play at the wrong time. Or maybe even the whole set comes up, and you're looking into the back of the theatre, costume changes and all that.

So as I was kin-hinning* along there, I thought, "Well, this is great, you know." Not only that I go out and, with no debate, head straight onto the wrong road, in the wrong direction, but when that becomes clear, just turn around and go the other direction. When you do that, especially when you do it with your eyes wide open, you get to see all the magic — you get to see how everything really works. When we waste our time worrying, first of all, about which is the right way to go, and then agonizing over having gone the wrong way, or whatever, we miss the magic — the magic not only of what we see as we're going down the wrong road, but especially when we double back and get on the right road.

It was exactly like spiritual practice.

❂

---

*Kin-hin is Zen walking meditation, very slow half-steps.

Your Own Salvation

Before trying to guide others, be your own guide first.

The Dhammapada

Cheri: When you're right there in the present and have that experience of dropping it all, and there's that peace and joy and clarity, it is magic. One of the hardest places for me in monastic training — and I bet if I look closely I'll find it's still hard for me on some level — is that it seems irresponsible to just drop it all and come back to the peace. You know, people are dying. People are starving and freezing to death and being tortured and having bombs dropped on them — we know all these things are going on, and more. So it can seem lacking in compassion to just drop your reactions to all of that and to come back to a sense of peace.

Q: But that doesn't necessarily mean that you do nothing, does it? Because it seems that only by ending your own suffering and reaching that peace can the clarity arise so you can see what is to be done.

A: I would suggest that even if you did nothing with that clarity, it is still not irresponsible to end your own suffering and to experience peace.

Q: That's hard for me. I just read that all that is needed for evil to prevail is for good people to do nothing. So on the one hand, I like to think that all I can do is be the most centered I can be, to live my life in the world from that position. But on the other, I think, well, I may be working on being a good person, but people have been doing that for centuries, and the misery just goes right on.

A: And yet, what would the level of misery be if nobody was

working on being a good person?

Q: Well, certainly in my own life it would be even higher.

A: An analogy I like is this. You find yourself in a building that's on fire. Nobody inside the building seems interested in having that information. You run around frantically trying to tell everybody, and they don't care. They're focused on what they're doing, they're busy, they're having a good time, they don't want to know. You could beat them over the head and try to drag them outside and be just as upset and frightened as you project they will be as soon as they realize what's happening. Or — you could simply find the exits and open the doors, then wait to be of assistance when everybody catches on that the building is burning.

If you abandon your own experience of peace out of a sense of obligation to be where everybody else is, I would suggest that you give up your only real possibility to be helpful. This is not something that all spiritual people would agree with. But this is what the Buddha taught. What he said was, you must each work out your own salvation diligently. We have one person to take care of every person: I am here to take care of me. I have the opportunity to end my suffering.

Here's another image I like. You know how on the plane the flight attendant stands up there and says if the cabin should lose pressure during the flight, the little masks will come down, and what you do is, put yours on first, then assist anybody around you who needs help. But if you don't put yours on and you start running up and down the aisles looking for people who need assistance, you're going to need assistance yourself, and you're going to be creating more problems.

So, first, end your own suffering. Then look around to see how you can help.

❂

42

Peace in the World: Interview

This interview was edited from a conversation recorded in February 1988 at the monastery. It began as my attempt to elicit from Cheri a comprehensive statement about how political activism fits into spiritual practice. I remember feeling then that she was not answering my questions. It was a long time before I understood the simple truth that what she said was not what I wanted to hear.

The interview not only turned out to be different from what I expected, but eventually opened my eyes to an utterly new perspective. The process of struggling to understand these issues — by observing my reactions, then looking deeper to see the underlying experience — has been one of the most difficult in my practice, and ultimately one of the most rewarding. It does seem to happen that way.

Q: How do you respond to the notion that Buddhism advocates passivity?

A: It's actually much easier to be what we call "active" than to follow the path taught in Buddhism, which goes against all our conditioning. What we think of as the active approach to the world involves these steps: I identify a problem outside myself, I act to solve it, then I don't have to change. The habit of looking for fault and placing blame is a strategy of egocentricity. Whether we blame others, or blame ourselves and feel guilty, it allows us to feel that we are doing something— but in fact, nothing changes.

The common thread is that either way keeps me at the center of the universe, and if I'm here and it's all out there, I don't have to take responsibility. It's much harder to stay with everything you don't want to accept, and to be compassionate with that. That is very hard. And that is the process we work with in Buddhism.

Q: How can we use our actions in the world as part of our

spiritual practice?

A: It's tricky, given our conditioning. We have to avoid the tendency to see our actions as self-denying, which, again, reinforces the sense of separate self. For example, if you take as a goal to love everyone, you must not forget that "everyone" includes you. We are all part of it all. To see "them" as deserving or requiring help and myself as otherwise perpetuates the duality. On the other hand, if you see a problem and can accept it as yours — without blaming yourself — then you can focus on what's really happening. What's going on? Why is it a problem? What am I clinging to? What don't I want to happen?

When you encounter a difficult person, let us say, in your quest to love everyone, you can notice your feelings of resistance, dislike, whatever. Just look at those feelings; observe those feelings with equanimity, remembering that you are one of the people to be loved. If you are honest, you will see how the qualities you dislike arise in yourself, rather than being "out there." What you see is your own projection. And if you watch carefully, you will see that there is a reason for everything. Something happened to cause everything that you are, and once you see why you are the way you are and how that all works — love, understanding, and compassion are the result. So, once you open your heart to what you find in yourself, it doesn't matter whether what you experience in this other person is true of them or not.

Q: So the effort involved is in the looking, rather than in trying to love.

A: Trying to make ourselves love people doesn't work, which is why we do it: we can grit our teeth and struggle and strain, none of which is any threat at all to egocentricity. In fact, it fully supports the sense of a separate self. But *looking* is not effortful in the same way. It requires only the effort to pay attention, but it's actually simple — it's just seeing what is. And when we don't want to see what is, it's looking at that, too. And when we have a better idea about what we should be doing, we look at that. If we can keep the heart open with acceptance to everything that is, each time we look, we practice compassion. Looking and acceptance are the same thing.

Q: Let me ask a question about power . . .

A: Before you do, let me say that I don't think we have the power to do anything to anyone else.

Q: But if one person can harm another one physically, isn't that . . . ?

A: I understand that it *appears* as if one person has "power" and another does not, that one is the oppressor and one is the victim. But no matter what happens to me, my experience of it is up to me. Other people cannot control my experience. We each have the power to determine our own experience of whatever happens, even if what happens is physical harm or death. Once we understand that, we can let go the idea that ends justify means.

If we weren't so invested in not understanding this, history would have taught us a long time ago that we don't get ends that are different from means. The process is everything. Not just the "journey is as important as the destination" way of looking at life, but how something is — is how it is. We won't create peace through violent methods.

Q: Couldn't I do something to somebody with a pretty good expectation of how they would react?

A: If you want to bank on the beliefs and assumptions that are culturally agreed upon, then, yes, a good deal of the time you'll be right. But the fact that many of us are in agreement about these things doesn't mean they're true. For example, if you spit on someone, the reaction will most likely be one of displeasure. But that doesn't mean that the act itself causes the displeasure. It's that we all respond to conditioning that says that to be spat upon is insulting and unacceptable, something that shouldn't happen. And what we look at in this practice is that our conditioning is the problem, not the external events.

Q: So we have to work on ourselves first.

A: While remembering that self-improvement doesn't work. There's a tendency to think we have to become perfect in order to see what is true. But our notions of perfection are conditioned, too; they're different for every society. We take our inability to meet those conditioned standards as signs of our imperfection — while it's the beliefs themselves that make us feel imperfect. Our job is simply to learn to see, not worrying about who we are. As long as we're trying to improve ourselves we'll be sure we have a self to improve. Egocentricity loves self-improvement.

Q: And you can't begin to see until you let go some of the conditioning.

A: Exactly. Because we're so focused on it — on trying to make our beliefs fit into what's going on that there's no possibility of simply being present to the moment. This practice is grounded in the understanding that you don't have to make what you believe fit into the present moment: you can simply drop it, forget it, just get here, right now, be present to what is.

Q: How does power fit into this?

A: You've got me.

Q: It's not — it's not a concept you deal with?

A: It really isn't. But I'm curious — you don't happen to have a dictionary with you, do you?

Q: Somehow it didn't occur to me to bring a dictionary to a place that doesn't have electricity . . .

A: It would be interesting to see how power is defined. I suppose we could think of power in terms of taking responsibility. I like to say that any of us can do anything, and we can, if we are willing to take full responsibility for our lives. There is a tendency to let the teacher do spiritual practice so we won't have to. It would work so much better if we acknowledge that the "teacher" is someone in whose presence we feel something in our hearts that we want to pursue, and we can learn from that person who walks ahead of us on the path, but without any dependency or expectation. We each have to do it for ourselves. It's the teaching, not the teacher, that matters.

Q: Is this why you aren't seeking ordination or dharma transmission and the like?

A: Yes. We work together here with the teachings, but without lineages and titles. If you're willing to study with someone without credentials, you've taken the first step toward accepting responsibility, which is essential to this practice. Taking responsibility for oneself may seem scary, but only until we realize that nothing can happen to us. We have to die, of course, but we can't make a mistake, we can't lose, we can't go wrong, as long as we pay attention.

Here are three things I wish for everybody: *Pay attention to everything. Accept all that is. Believe nothing.* As long as you're doing that, nothing can happen to you. If you're going along and step in a hole and fall flat on your face, you've learned a great deal. Now, if you have a preconceived notion that it's not okay to have this happen, you'll be unhappy. And eventually you'll be afraid to go anywhere, because you might step in a hole at any point. This is where many of us find ourselves. Because of our conditioning, because of what has happened in the past or what we are afraid might happen, we live in fear. Terrified of doing it wrong — that's the big one for most people.

But of course that's already doing it wrong: living in fear is doing it wrong.

Q: Are you saying that nothing can happen to you that is not useful in your own liberation?

A: Yes.

Q: And the opportunity to observe your own suffering is particularly beneficial.

A: Extremely beneficial. We project out of our own fear, insecurity, deprivation, you name it, and see someone doing something we don't like, then want them to change it so we don't have that experience any longer. But there's another way of looking at it: instead of seeing it as "something wrong" and taking it personally, you can simply learn from it.

Q: I want to ask how political activism can be reconciled with Buddhism. On the one hand you've got the vow to save all sentient beings, which sounds activist, but on the other — well, there's the notion of Buddhist pacifism and acceptance of the status quo.

A: Before I acted, I'd want to look. To look deeply at myself and understand what's really going on *here*. With me.

Q: What exactly are you looking for?

A: If I see in the world that which is harmful, or evil, or dangerous, or needs to be corrected, it behooves me to find those places within myself — because I am projecting those qualities out from myself. It would be good for me to look at what could be corrected within myself before I go about attempting to change things outside myself.

Q: But sometimes you have to act on insufficient information.

A: Oh, indeed, yes. Most of the time, I'd venture to say.

Q: And if you don't act quickly, you hand over power to others who may act in a really destructive way — I'm thinking of the Holocaust, terrorism, child abuse. Let's take an example. What if you know a child is being abused next door? It's a clear-cut problem: you know who the victim is and who the oppressor is.

A: I'm not that clear about it. I don't really know that there's only one victim — so-called. It seems to me that there might be a whole houseful of "victims."

Q: Still, you'd call the authorities.

A: Consider another possibility. What if you just put to one side your beliefs and assumptions, your need to keep your universe in order by knowing who is the oppressor and who's the victim, and your need to protect yourself by deferring to an outside authority? You might just go over there and get to know these people, find out who they are and what their story is, spend time with them, be with them — and at the end of a year of opening your heart fully to them, see if you could be so sure who's playing what role.

Q: But while you're . . .

A: I know you think I'm not answering the question. But just let me make this point: whether or not you act is less important than *how* — the attitude with which you approach your activism.

Q: But while you're meditating or working on your attitude or whatever, the world is being destroyed. Or a child is being hurt.

A: But who is destroying the world? Who is hurting that child? And who is the child who is hurting?

Q: Well — who?

A: That's something we might want to look at. I couldn't put it better than the Bible does. Before you attempt to remove the mote in your neighbor's eye, remove the beam from your own. Not that you need to feel humiliated or inadequate because of your imperfections — no, no, no! It's simply that you are not seeing clearly.

Q: You're saying you need to take your own situation into account?

A: We do well to include ourselves in our view of the world. The point of all this is to open one's heart — to be in the moment with the heart as open as possible, with the mind as clear as possible, then to look and see what is so, from the point of view of what is most compassionate for all. We're all in this in the very same way. All of us victims, and all of us oppressors.

Q: So — how do you act?

A: You act according to what seems so in the moment. But you can't quit paying attention. It's not as if once you've seen the truth, you've got it down once and for all and can proceed straight to nirvana. What is true in this moment doesn't necessarily apply to other situations. Rules for life do not appear in a form that can be posted on your refrigerator door for future reference. The *seeing itself* is the point. When you're *seeing in the moment* you operate out of that. And there is no "you" separate from what is seen, there's just seeing — and the seeing and the acting are one.

Q: This sounds like the formlessness of Zen. Or passivity — the passivity of Buddhism.

A: Or we might call it taking full responsibility for oneself. And for the state of the universe.

Q: Are you saying those are the same?

A: Yes. Small scale or global, the process is the same, if what , we're talking about is freedom, ending suffering.

Q: Aren't there circumstances in which what we might call plain old human nature would make you intervene in a situation involving other people? By offering help, say?

A: As long as we understand that everything we do is for ourselves, I don't think we get too far afield. What confuses things is the belief that "I" can do something for "you." That's not how it works. Even if I'm doing it because I'd feel too awful

51

not doing it, I'm still doing it for me.

Q: How can standing up against an atrocity be selfish? For example, opposing a radioactive waste dump is acting in behalf of everybody . . .

A: Everybody who is nearby, anyway. But were local people fighting it when it was going somewhere else? I'm not saying there's anything wrong with that — it's exactly how things work — but I'm saying let's not make it more noble than it is. Let's not turn it into Truth and Justice. Because that's not what's going on.

It comes back to projection: this is what I want. My version of justice, my idea of compassion, my kind of peace, which I feel entitled to impose on you. But in this practice my job is to look at right here, to see what's going on with me, where I am suffering, violent, harmful — and resolve those issues within myself.

Keep in mind that I am talking only from a spiritual perspective. My teacher used to say — and I often quote this, it's one of my favorite things he ever said — that if we blow up this world, we'll also blow up the only ones who care. Not a tragedy. So to justify things I want to do by invoking a higher cause — for the good of the world, for humanity, for the future — well, go back to the Bible. What profit is it if you gain the world and lose your soul? You can "lose your soul" just as easily trying to gain truth, justice, peace, compassion, and so on for the world. But when you really get clear, the seeing and doing itself are your reward.

Q: Virtue is its own reward.

A: It is true, and nobody wants to hear it. Another favorite quotation of mine is from R. H. Blythe: "Everybody knows that they need to sell everything they have and give the money to the poor and forgive their enemies, and nobody wants to hear that, so we keep asking questions." These acts are unacceptable to egocentricity; to do these things you must be in a place of compassion. From that place, goodness is its own compensation. If you're living a life of goodness, you don't need anything else. But because we're not living a life of goodness, but "doing good" to meet our own needs and rationalizing that by calling it sacrifice or service or good deeds, then we want to be compensated for it.

Q: What do you mean by "living a life of goodness"?

A: I mean *being* goodness. Once your effort is focused on opening your heart, staying with your heart open through everything you encounter, and you see that everything you do is for your own spiritual training, you're much less dangerous. But when we want something other than what is, no matter how noble we tell ourselves it is, we step into that cycle of suffering that compounds the ignorance, greed, and hatred that exists in the world.

From a spiritual point of view, the externals are not what matters. We focus on externals because they dramatize for us what's going on internally. We're karmically drawn to those circumstances that help maintain our sense of who we are, that support the particular illusion of separateness that we identify with — identify as "I." Then we blame those circumstances for our life experience. But when we learn to look closely — and that's what we practice on this path — certain ways of acting, or not acting, will become obvious as more helpful than the way we've been doing it. One unhelpful way that some people see pretty quickly is the tendency to blame others for our own experience — to project out onto the world what we feel, or fear, or want, and to disregard the fact that it's ours, it's us. If it's out *there*, we can tell ourselves we aren't responsible.

Q: Like the radioactive waste — everybody wants to dump it somewhere else. Nobody wants to claim it, so it stays around, contaminating everything.

A: Really karmic, when you think about it.

Q: I still want to ask, if you're going to undertake political action, what is the attitude you bring to that?

A: Well, as St. Augustine says, "Love, and do as you will." Not grit your teeth and tell yourself you should love your enemy when you don't. But love that enemy within you, for whom you alone are responsible. Find in yourself and learn to embrace both the victim and the oppressor.

This is the trick, you see, in our vow to save all sentient beings. Once you understand nonseparateness, it is clear that the saving is all done right here, within oneself. If you want to talk about power, that's where our power lies. Where one begins in acting to improve the world is — right here. One's own action. That's what karma means. One comes to meditation as a way of knowing oneself. This [pointing to herself] — *this* is where it happens.

As long as we are concerned about what the other side is doing, we will always have war. If we want peace, we need to be willing to lay it all down. Then we can move from a place of having resolved things so completely within ourselves that we can afford to be generous, going so far as to say to the other person, "Now — what is it that you need?"

What the Buddha talked about, what it comes down to, is this: if every person took responsibility for being the way they want the world to be, we wouldn't have a problem. That's why we can't say that the problem in the world is that people are sick or that people are hungry. Or, that the problem is that people are wealthy, or selfish. Altering externals is never going to work, because the problem is our own ignorance, wanting

54

something other than what is. The biggest irony of all is that we are afraid to let go because we are afraid the world will be awful — and the only reason the world is awful is that we are clinging to our notions of how the world should be.

It is always going to be the way it is. And when we want something other than that, we get ourselves into the cycle of suffering that compounds all of the ignorance, the greed, the hatred that exist in the world. But when we wake up and see that what is, is, and that our resisting it and hating it and suffering over it is not going to change it, we become free to do whatever we want to do.

We talk about karma as a wheel, our conditioned reactions leading inevitably to suffering as the wheel turns. What we learn in this practice is how to bring that wheel to a stop. Then we begin to turn the wheel in a different direction, away from suffering.

✿

ENDING OUR SUFFERING: STUDENTS

Our suffering over not getting what we want is like a fishhook in soft flesh. If nothing tugs on it (that is, if we're getting our way), we can pretty much ignore it. Slight pressure on one of those conditioned responses results in some discomfort — but nothing we can't handle, we tell ourselves. A sharp jerk of the hook may cause acute pain and leave a wound. A serious blow to the ego is like a long, hard pull that tears through living tissue, mutilating our idea of ourselves, creating agonizing pain.

If we notice that this unbearable pain disappears when our attention is elsewhere, we may conclude that ending our suffering comes from not thinking about it. It takes little practice in meditation, however, to discover that not thinking is so much easier said than done as to not be worth the effort. At some point, our interest turns to removing the hook — that cruel instrument of our conditioning. The desire to eliminate the source of suffering, rather than to merely avoid its effects, is the beginning of spiritual practice.

Just as there are two schools of thought on the best way to remove a band-aid that stubbornly adheres to the skin, so is Zen divided between the sudden and the gradual approaches to stripping away egocentricity. The Soto tradition (in which Cheri trained) has no objection to sudden enlightenment, but offers an alternative: undoing our attachments — those stuck-tight habits of suffering — gently, one by one, to release our true nature, to uncover our joy.

The conversations that follow took place among about a dozen students. Most of them attended the Zen Center; two were from the San Francisco sitting group, and two were living at the monastery. The talks were mainly recorded during a weekend in February 1988 at the Villa Angelica convent in Carmel.

When the subject is release from suffering, and the process is to look that suffering in the face, there is no way to avoid talking about what is painful in life. And yet, sitting in a circle of lounge chairs in the courtyard, sporting visors and hats and sunglasses and sandals, surrounded by dazzling stucco walls and bright flowers, the breeze fragrant with pine and ocean, there was much to celebrate. Simply sharing the company of others who travel this path, who aim to step free from the trap of our conditioning, is in itself a deep pleasure.

These discussions represent the group's attempts to describe this practice — not by summarizing principles, but by recounting how the compassionate examination of one's experience opens new perspectives and new possibilities, by searching for words to describe specifically how this happens, by speaking openly about their lives. For a few of those present, the joy of freedom had become a sustaining flow; for some, a glimpsed reality; for others, a promise of what could be.

❂

Where We Start

Let no one think lightly of good and say. . . "Joy will not come
to me." Little by little a person becomes good, as a water pot
is filled by drops of water.

The Dhammapada

Greg: When I first came to the Center, I thought a lot about this question: why, since I was so smart, didn't things work out right in my life? I was sure there was something wrong with me, and I wanted to fix it through meditation.

Something happened right away that opened my eyes. When I first spoke to Cheri on the telephone, she said I could come to the introductory meditation workshop. She said there would be bells rung and people bowing, but not to worry about all that. I asked if it wouldn't be a problem if I didn't know what to do. And she said something like, "Well, you couldn't very well know how to do something you've never done before."

That really impressed me. I always wanted to make sure I knew what to do in advance, or I'd pretend I knew until I could figure out what the rules were, and then I'd act as if I'd known all along. The notion that you could be a beginner at some-thing — you could not know what to do and that was all right, you'd just go ahead and learn — that was a real revelation.

After that my question became, is it possible to *always* know what to do, no matter what situation you are in?

Cheri: The classic question: how can you know that what you're doing is right? But life is going to happen anyway, and if we get out of the way, if we can let go trying to figure it out so we can impose our will on it, things run much more smoothly. Whenever we have ideas of the right way and the wrong way, whenever we set up standards about how things should be, it doesn't work, because these ideas and standards are other than the way life is.

Jan: But there's such tremendous fear of letting go those ideas.

Cheri: We are afraid only because we see ourselves as separate. It is the *illusion* of separateness that causes us to suffer. It's that illusion of separateness that causes us to feel alone and isolated and abandoned and afraid. If it's me against the universe, I think I have to control everything. So there are all these questions. How can I make sure I'll do the right thing? How will I get what I need? When in fact, I would say, the only *real* need we have is unconditional love and acceptance.

Bhasa: Can't you give that to yourself?

Cheri: Oh, yes! That's the only way it can happen. But from the point of view of egocentricity, it's not possible to see that there is anything beyond egocentricity, which is maintained by all those wants, ideas, standards, beliefs, assumptions, and so on. Imagining not having those is like looking at your own death: I wouldn't be me.

So, who is this "me"? Where does egocentricity come from?

At a workshop I did last week a woman said, "Why are people mean for no reason, even to people they don't even know?" If we want to know the answer to that, we have to look at the whole picture. It's not as if here I was, perfectly innocent, and you were mean for no reason, and the world just began in that moment. When you look at it that way, what a sad little picture it is: I'm the victim, you're the villain.

But what if we look at both sides of it as coming from "before the beginning of beginningless time"? We might see that it's not her fault, because she's responding to something that happened to her, and the person who did that to her was responding to something that happened to him, and so on.

Then we might realize that both of us are coming from the same experience. We feel alone and frightened and victimized and inadequate in the world. We're trying to get what we need and we see other people as a threat to that: they all seem to have more than we have, or have a better chance than we have, or always know what is the right thing to do. We can't see that they experience life in exactly the same way we do because we're so focused on the idea of our own lack and deprivation that there's no way we can be sensitive to theirs.

If we understood that we're all in the same situation, then we would start taking care of one another. Automatically, we would feel safe, adequate, complete, and we would realize that whatever we have is plenty.

—

Cheri: Buddhism says that your conditioning didn't start at birth. That's why we use these wild phrases like "You are everything that it has taken to produce you since before the beginning of beginningless time." You get a sense of the magnitude of the conditioning that's involved, why the same patterns get repeated over and over and over.

That's what we mean by karma. Karma is just action. There isn't good karma or bad karma, there's just karma. There's just action and the result of that action. When one thing happens, another thing usually happens as a result. We are conditioned toward certain tendencies, attitudes, beliefs, behaviors. We act out of that conditioning because, of course, once we're conditioned, we don't know there's an alternative. So we act out of what has happened before, and that conditions us further, then we continue to act that way, and that conditions us further . . . okay?

Karmic experience is often likened to a wheel, and the wheel turns with this lumbering, laborious movement, taking out everything in its path. That's what the motion of karma is like.

June: When you say that, I see a scene from *2001: A Space Odyssey,* the circular space station that looks like a wheel slowly turning through space. The soundtrack in the film was a Viennese waltz, but the sound I hear comes from *Star Trek IV,* that steady dull roar that just fills the whole universe. That's how I see karma, and I see me there trying to stop it. And it seems impossible.

Cheri: Well, it is. It is impossible for me to stop it. Does everyone know why?

Peter: Because "me" is only defined by the wheel going round.

Cheri: When there is no "me," there will be no wheel of karma.

June: So I only have to stop my own wheel.

Cheri: Yes, that ends the suffering.

June: Oh — I can picture that. It's quite a bit smaller.

Cheri: Although it doesn't feel that way when you're being crushed under it. Spiritual training is a process for bringing that movement to a stop. That's the first part of it, ending those cycles. The second is turning away from suffering.

✺

Turning Away From Suffering

The cause of our sorrow is ego delusion.
From dark path to dark path we've wandered in darkness—
how can we be free from the wheel of samsara?

Zen Master Hakuin

Cheri: In ending suffering, one part of the process is bringing old behaviors to a stop. We approach that in a gentle way — not making ourselves stop doing something, but resolving it, letting it go, so it simply doesn't exist any longer, compared to suppressing it or avoiding it.

Bonnie: That's where meditation is practice for life. When I sit and let the thoughts come and go, I'm able to step back from it all, and that becomes a habit. So there's almost always part of me that isn't totally involved in whatever's happening and doesn't really believe the soap opera, the drama of it all. Other parts of me can be miserable, but there's a solid little knot of something that doesn't get drawn in.

Cheri: Once you've had that experience, it's like a little voice in the back of your head says, "This is simply a conditioned response." But it takes work to just allow that to be instead of saying, "I shouldn't be doing this, I know better." Because — well, why not do that?

Bonnie: Because judging comes from thinking it should be this way or that way rather than simply seeing what is.

Cheri: Yes. Any hint of wanting to get rid of something means I'm just pushing it away, which is not at all the same as "letting it go" or resolving it.

Here's something I like to encourage people to do. Let's say I've identified something that's causing me suffering. I know

I should let go of it, but I don't want to — you know that awful guilt-producing place? "What kind of person am I? I've done all the work of seeing clearly what it is, and now I don't want to let go of it." So, let go of it. Stop doing it. See how that feels, see what happens. Then — do it. Do that very thing, pay close attention, and see what happens then. Watch really, really closely. Then do this: whenever you want to do this thing, don't do it; whenever you don't want to do it, do it. And periodically when you want to do it, do it, and when you don't want to do it, don't do it. Above all, *pay attention*. Because it — whatever "it" is — is almost never what we think it is.

Jan: I'm not sure I understand. I can't see how to apply "do it when you don't want to." The way I'm looking at it is, how do I quit doing it?

Cheri: No, no. Oh, no. What's an example of something somebody struggles with?

Greg: Junk food.

Cheri: Food. Compulsive eating. Okay. Let's say I love sugar, and I could eat sugar twenty-four hours a day. But I realize that sugar's not good for me. It doesn't even make me feel good, and I know that. If I say, "Okay, I'm not going to eat sugar, and that's that," I get very tense and determined, I go to a hypnotist, I begin an exercise plan — whatever. It becomes a contest. I last a week, two weeks maybe, and then I'm doing it again. And hating myself. I know it's bad for me, and still I do it. Why don't I have any willpower?

Now, this is a spiritual issue we're talking about. It doesn't have anything to do with sugar. The point is that how I do this relationship with sugar is how I do everything. It's how I do my whole life, and that's what I want to find out: how I do ignorance, how I do delusion, denial, suffering, resistance, hatred, punishing, rewarding, withholding.

I may think I'm pretty clear about what happens when I eat sugar, but it would probably be helpful to sit down and eat it with full awareness. Not run in, eat it, and run off to do something else, but sit there, eat a candy bar, and watch what happens. Watch for the next two hours and see what happens. Then, *not* eat sugar for a day and watch what happens. If I'm serious about it I might even go on a meditation retreat to do this. Go away for the weekend, where there's no pressure, nothing else going on but me and this sugar addiction. Then there'll be times when I don't want to eat sugar. That's a good time to eat it! It's like one of the quit-smoking techniques: smoke an entire carton of cigarettes. Takes a lot of the fun out of it. But the important thing is to look at what's happening. Who, what part of me, wants sugar? What's going on with that part of myself? What's trying to control what? How am I rewarding myself and punishing myself? In other words, examine this behavior under all possible circumstances, until there is nothing you don't know about your relationship to sugar.

It sounds very controlled, but if you take decisions and will out of it, it's really a process of letting go. All of those situations will occur — wanting it and getting it, wanting it and not getting it, not wanting it and getting it, and so on — and if you're willing to go along with whatever comes up for you, you'll see exactly how you work.

So, something is going on that's making us unhappy, or we're acting in a way that we don't approve of. We're suffering, we don't like it. This is the conditioned response: we're on automatic pilot. This is the K-word—karma. So there I am: this is what has happened, this is what I think, this is what I feel. I'm looking at my emotional reaction. What next?

Jean: Step back and see where it's coming from? Who it's coming from?

Cheri: Yes. And the "who" it's coming from, for us, in this practice, is a really important element, because all of the aspects of ourselves, all of the conditioned aspects of ourselves, have their own conditioned responses.

We call these aspects of ourselves "subpersonalities." That's just a concept we use to get an intuitive sense of how all of this happens. The whole notion of subpersonalities is a model for describing conditioned responses. Looking at a particular subpersonality, I can see that I'm conditioned to respond to a given situation in a certain way, and another subpersonality shows me that I'm conditioned to respond in another way, depending on which set of conditioned responses is currently operating. So, subpersonalities constitute our conditioned identity.

Have you noticed that generally it is an emotional reaction you don't like that catches your attention? Yes. The feeling of "not-liking" is helpful in our spiritual growth because it alerts us that there's something to work with.

Now: here I am in an emotional reaction that I don't like. What do I do?

Peter: You see how it feels in your body.

Cheri: You go right from being aware of your emotional reaction to being aware of the sensation. And when you're paying attention to what's happening with your body, you are also watching the kinds of thoughts that go with that. When we talk about seeing, or paying attention, we're talking about watching what's going on with us physically, what's going on with us mentally, what we're saying to ourselves, what we believe. We're watching the emotional reaction to that, and of course we're usually talking to ourselves about that, as well. "I don't like this, I shouldn't be this way, why am I doing this?" And then the action that we're going to choose: "I should have done that, but I didn't. And so now here I am ... okay, then,

I'll leave town. I'll apologize. I'll quit my job. I'll get a divorce." Whatever you think you have to do under these circumstances.

One of the things that helps us is that, since the whole thing is conditioned, this scenario doesn't come up just once. Oh, no. It keeps happening; we get back to the very same place again and again. To take the example of sugar addiction: if I feel bad, I want to eat sugar. An automatic response, which finally catches my attention about the fortieth or fiftieth or hundredth time. Then I realize, "This sounds like a program I do."

Staying with the discomfort, to get to the point of letting go, takes a great deal of willingness, because we want to bail out. But the bailing out is what enables us to continue to do this over and over and over again. The not staying with it is what perpetuates it.

Jean: When I do stay with it, I usually find that what I think of as pain is just resistance to pain, and fear is just resistance to fear. I haven't even gotten to the actual issue yet, and already I'm resisting the pain or the fear.

Bonnie: When I identify the subpersonality that's having the problem, if I'm angry, say, and I'm able to accept that, then if I can find out whether it's coming from pain or fear (it's always one of those two), the secondary emotion is totally obliterated. Seeing what's really going on underneath makes the anger just go away, because the focus is on the deeper, more primary experience.

Cheri: Not that you're trying to get rid of it — it's just that paying attention opens up a new door.

The second part is turning the wheel in the other direction so that we move away from suffering and toward goodness, so the action from that point on doesn't have the harmful effects

67

that the previous action does. From a Buddhist perspective, greed, hate, and delusion are the conditioning that has been operating in our lives. We bring that to a halt by living in a way that moves instead toward wisdom, love, and compassion.

Here's a simple example of how we create suffering for ourselves by resisting what is: taking the weather personally. It's raining, and I don't like it. I don't want this to be happening. That windstorm we just had up at the monastery — our reaction is to think that something is terribly wrong — oh, no, the tent is supposed to be on the ground, not up in the trees! But no need to take it personally: the wind just blows, the sun shines. It rains, it quits raining. That's how life is, and we can let all of that happen. We can let it come up, and we can let it pass away — no problem.

Do we ever get used to anger in the same way? Anger comes up; we have to have a big emotional response to it, we have to make a decision about it, we have to decide what it says about who I am, what's going on with me, why I did that, this is wrong, instead of — ah, anger. Ah, rain.

❁

Willingness To See

*The Lord Tathagata [the Buddha] took the handkerchief with
the knots still tied in it and tugged at it in a blind, foolish
way that only served to tighten the knots and asked Ananda
if the knots could be unloosened in that way.*

Ananda replied:— No, my Lord.

*Then the Lord tugged at the knots in another wrong way
and again asked if the knots could be unloosed in that way.*

Ananda replied:— No, my Lord.

*The Lord Buddha said:—I have tried now that way and
now this way, but with no success in unloosening the knots.
How would you untie them, Ananda?*

*Ananda replied:— My Lord, I would first study the knot
and find out how it was tied, then it could easily be untied.*

*The Lord Buddha was pleased with this reply and said:—
Right you are, Ananda! If you wish to untie a knot, you must
first understand how it was tied.*

The Surangama Sutra

Cheri: When we say "turning away from suffering" we don't
mean pushing it away. What if we look at suffering as simply
resistance to what is, wanting something other than what is,
having the ability to imagine that there is something other
than what is and wanting that, clinging to that notion?

Jeannie: You know the story about the man who is hanging
from the cliff and there's the tiger underneath him and he's
clinging to a vine and mice are chewing it and he's about to
drop, and he sees a strawberry and has a good time eating it.
I finally got the point of that story. I always thought the
situation you were in determined how you felt, so it was just
automatic that bad feelings go along with bad circumstances.
The story about the strawberry suggests that that isn't necessarily true, which seemed strange to me. Here is somebody in
the worst situation you could imagine, and he doesn't say,
"Well, I guess I've got to feel awful about this." He sees a
chance to feel all right for a second, and he takes it.

Cheri: It does seem strange, doesn't it? That's what gives a religion like this a bad reputation. It's not normal to enjoy something when everything's awful. Clearly, what any normal person would say is, "Who cares about a strawberry at a time like this?" Unfortunately, we tend to say that about almost every moment in life. It's always too awful to enjoy the strawberry.

Sylvia: I wonder how many people actually realize that they are suffering. I know I did a lot of denying about that. It never occurred to me that I was really suffering. Suffering seemed like what happens to people who are starving or poor, who are deprived in some circumstantial way. I think the point that suffering is an attitude of mind is a novel idea for a lot of people. If you tell people that this process is designed to end suffering, they say, "Oh, well, that has nothing to do with me. I'm not suffering. Life is difficult sometimes, but it doesn't count as suffering."

Cheri: If you consider the qualities of your true nature — wisdom, love, compassion, joy, peace — and if we define suffering as everything other than that, it gets a little clearer, doesn't it? That's exactly what the Buddha was talking about. He wasn't talking about losing both legs and now you're really suffering.

Suffering includes everything from dissatisfaction to displeasure to loss of life and limb and utter misery. Suffering is there at the moment when you get exactly what you want and discover you're still not happy. "Is that all there is?" we wonder, because that didn't make everything all right after all. What now? Get another degree? Get a better car? A bigger house? A different relationship? You can stay ahead of the game if you play your cards right, because the rush you feel from each of those things can carry you for another few years or so.

It's kind of fun to look at how often we change things. Let's take three major categories: what you do for a living, who you're in relationship to, and your material possessions. If you look at how often you change those, can you begin to get a sense of your basic pattern? Maybe a two-year cycle? Or every four years? Just review your life and see if you can get a sense of that pattern, when it all begins to close in, when it's time to change something, because the change stirs everything up, throws us off balance for a little bit — we're involved, we're busy, we have something to think about, there isn't that boring sensation that there's nothing more than this.

Now, if we can just begin to look at how we do this, to pay attention to these patterns, to be willing to see it all . . .

June: We see how we suffer.

Cheri: Exactly. But — no guilt, no blame, no resistance. Just paying attention, and faith.

Peter: Faith is the hardest thing for me to understand.

Cheri: It might be helpful to talk about the *willingness to see* and how faith can grow out of that experience. What is it like, finding the willingness to stop what we've been doing and simply look at what is?

Jeannie: I think it can happen when you see clearly that what you've been doing doesn't work. But once you've said, "Okay, I'm willing to see," it can look like things are worse instead of better, because you see all the stuff that you hadn't been able to face before.

Cheri: Yes — in this practice we talk about "going farther and faring worse." At first, when your perception is very gross, you consider the things you look at to be very subtle. Then your

71

perception becomes more subtle, and what you see in yourself is obviously more gross. So how do you maintain the willingness to stay with that?

Jeannie: Even though you see all this awful stuff about yourself more and more clearly, you still have a sense that you're not living in quite the same way as you did before.

Cheri: So there's a little hope in that?

Jeannie: Yes. At least you know the suffering is not just piling higher and deeper the way it used to be. Every now and then you get this little glimmer of a thought that maybe you're making your way through, instead of spinning your wheels.

Bonnie: Somewhere along the way I realized that in this practice, learning wisdom, love, and compassion for all beings means including this one [pointing to herself]. That was a big step, because until I was able to look at myself with a little less judgment and a little more compassion, it was just too painful to look.

Peter: I agree. I've been stuck in that spot. I'd tell myself, I've spent time in quite a few Zen centers, I've read fifty books on Zen, I've been sitting for years, I've been doing retreats, I've been listening to lectures, I should know what this is all about. So how come I still get angry, frustrated, depressed? For a long time, all those feelings seemed to stand in the way of my Zen practice. Now I understand that all that *is* the practice. That was like a light switch going on, because now I see where to put my effort. Paying attention to all this stuff going on *is* the process.

Cheri: After we've seen a few things, we begin to realize that there's a fairly predictable process. Something happens. Our predisposition is to say, "Oh, no, I don't want to look at this, it's going to be awful, it's going to show things about me that I don't want to know." But our experience tells us that that's a normal reaction — and we don't have to believe it. So we can go right ahead and look.

The moment you do that, the moment you drop all the resistance and just open yourself up, there's freedom. There's that immediate sense of release and joy that comes from letting go and accepting something as it is. Then the information starts coming in, because when there's no resistance, there's a complete clarity, and I can see things as they are. There's even an excitement with it. Almost, "Oh, that's like this, and that's like that, and that's because of this, and I can see how it all goes together." After we do that process a several dozen times or several hundred or thousand times or whatever it takes, the resistance begins to fall away.

If we can add an element of humor, so much the better. Having a lightness about it puts us in a position to see more clearly. "I'm ready," I tell myself. "I know it's going to happen again, and I'm just going to watch." I'm sure you can feel the difference between the attitude of, "Oh, god, I don't want that to happen, I'm going to blow it again, I've blown it every other time," and, "I'm ready. Ah — yes. Here it is. Again. Yes."

❂

Sitting

You should pay attention to the fact that even the Buddha Sakyamuni had to practice zazen [sitting meditation] for six years. It is also said that Bodhidharma had to do zazen at Shao-lin temple for nine years . . . . Since these ancient sages were so diligent, how can present-day trainees do without the practice of zazen?

Zen Master Dogen

Cheri: Sitting in meditation is a wonderful opportunity to grasp your willingness. Do you know what I mean by that?

Jeannie: It means to me that meditation is a way of practicing that very hard letting go of things. In meditation, all these interesting thoughts come up, and I practice letting them go. I see how very unwilling I am to do that, how much I want to think about them. I see the wrench, the real sense of loss, when I decide not to think of whatever is there.

Cheri: And to return the attention to following the breath, or whatever meditation technique you are using — to come back right here. It takes tremendous effort to be present, to sit up straight, to get into meditation posture, and stay there. It seems as if the only thing we're ready to go along with is suffering. If we put as much into sitting as we do into suffering — who can tell?

In sitting practice we find the willingness to stay there, even when the mind starts to wander off into all those fascinating, seductive thought patterns. Willingness not to wander, not to drift, not to fall into the old conditioned habit patterns of suffering, but to stay right there, present and attentive and awake.

But it has to be in a way that doesn't turn into punishing yourself — that's essential. If you find yourself wandering off, come back to the breath, renew that effort, commit again. No need to say, "What's the matter with me?" That's three steps down the road in the other direction. But, "Oh, this is hard. I have to watch much more closely, because I was way off there even before I knew it. But here I am again. And I'm going to stay here."

Jan: I've found that sitting strengthens my willingness to challenge my own beliefs, to see if what seems like absolute truth really is. Physical pain is a good example. You're sitting, and you feel this screaming inside, "I can't take this anymore!" But if you are not identified with that voice, you can simply ask if that really is the case. Is it true that I cannot stand this? Just doing that once is amazing, and then you want to try it again and again.

Cheri: One thing we can remember is that we've never experienced a pain we could not stand. We're living proof that we survived all those pains. So when the voice says, "I can't stand it," we don't have to believe it.

What if I don't move? What's going to happen? Will I die on the spot? Will I lose my mind? It's important to find out what that means. What we discover is that the voice is saying, "I don't want to sit through this." Next we may hear part of us saying, "I choose not to stand this." Then the next step can be, "But I do choose to stand it." We can ask, "Who is the 'I' who can't stand it?" rather than identifying with it and believing it. Because when that identification happens, we're in big trouble.

Do you see the importance of this? As long as you believe you can't stand it, you're a victim. It's as simple as that. As soon as you see through that belief, you cannot remain a victim. It's not possible.

Jan: But it takes tremendous courage to do it. The littlest thing, like pain when you're sitting — it doesn't seem small then at all. It seems like it takes everything I have to stay with it.

Cheri: It takes more than you have. That's the magic of it.

June: How do you keep from making it a contest?

Cheri: If you make it a contest, you'll lose. And then you'll be in the next round.

June: But that's the result of making it a contest. There's no "how?"

Cheri: No. Although one effective method is to drop the contest and come back here. Because the contest can't maintain itself without a great deal of cooperation.

Carole: Also, by letting go, I'm giving that part of myself what she wants. That part really cannot stand it. Dropping the resistance, stepping back from the struggle and disidentifying from it frees the part of me who can't stand it. So I'm taking care of her. There's a difference between what she wants — which is to get up and leave the meditation hall — and what she needs, which is not to stay stuck, to get free from the experience of "I can't stand it." So in letting go, I'm freeing her, meeting that need with compassion.

Cheri: Right. So she doesn't have to suffer.

❖

How We Abandon Our Hearts

Universal Mind is thoroughly pure in its essential nature,
subsisting unchanged and free from faults of impermanence,
undisturbed by egoism, unruffled by distinctions, desires and
aversions. Universal Mind is like a great ocean, its surface
ruffled by waves and surges but its depths remaining forever
unmoved. In itself it is devoid of personality and all that
belongs to it, but by reason of the defilement upon its face it
is like an actor and plays a variety of parts, among which a
mutual functioning takes place and the mind-system arises.
The principle of intellection becomes divided and mind, the
functions of mind, the evil out-flowings of mind, take on
individuation.

The Lankavatara Scripture

Cheri: In this practice of ending suffering, we can see suffering as a circle, a continuous process. There's the conditioning that results in our turning away from our hearts, because we assume we have to do that in order to survive. Then we begin to live from the perspective of greed, hate, and delusion, and to project greed, hate, and delusion out onto the world. We see our own attitudes everywhere we look, so those projections seem to be confirmed by the world, and we assume we have to do what the world is telling us, which is to live by our conditioned responses. The practice is to see through all this, back to our original nature of purity and goodness.

How did we turn away from that? How did we ever come to abandon our true selves? How does the conditioning happen, how does egocentricity arise? We all start out innocent, but with certain predispositions. As we grow, we are confronted with a choice: to stay with who we are, and our own innocence — our own true nature, if you will — or to identify with the authority figures who seem to have power over us, to have our survival in their hands. So, when there's something I need, and I ask for it, and my request is denied, the information I get from mother, father, whoever is providing for me is, "Only if you do what I require will I provide the love and nurturing and care and support that you need." So, I choose to leave the purity of my own heart and agree to do what is required by others in order to get my needs met.

There's no way not to make that choice away from ourselves toward society. Socialization is unavoidable. It is perfectly understandable that we chose as we did. It wasn't a mistake; we're not to be blamed for that. In fact, it was one of those non-choices, where in theory there's a choice, but our experience is such that no choice seems possible, and so we intelligently go with the program that enables us to survive.

That's the beginning of the process of turning away from our hearts and toward egocentricity, toward identification with the illusion of separateness. That process of identifying with the illusion of separateness contains in it deprivation, fear, abandonment, isolation, and guilt. I would guess that this is where the Garden of Eden story came from. It's about choosing knowledge over God, choosing egocentricity over one's true nature.

Once we believe ourselves to be separate from all that is, from that point on, we're projecting out onto the world our guilt, our bad feelings about ourselves, our anger and resentment, our hopelessness. We keep looking at our lives and asking ourselves, "How did I get into this? What am I going to do? How can I make the best of it?"—seeing life as a salvage operation, what we call in Buddhism "seeking better accommodation." You know, "Maybe if I had this, maybe if I had that, if I were really respectable, if I led a very good life, if I did something to help the world—wouldn't that make it better?"

It can be very hard for many people to see that this is merely projection of the fundamental attitudes of inadequacy that arise in the conditioning process. We tend to believe in our projections, until we start a practice like this and begin to look really closely at what's going on. One of the most difficult parts of projection is that one subpersonality projects, and then another one looks at the projection and denies it. For instance, maybe a judgmental part of me comes out and says, "Something or other is disgusting," and then another subpersonality says, "Can you see how you're like that?" And a different one steps in and says, in wide-eyed sincerity, "No" — and really can't see it, because the part who just had that experience is no longer there. That's why we have so much trouble catching ourselves, because often one part of us does something then goes away, and another part is there that really doesn't have that experience.

Jeannie: Projection is always hard for me because I look at somebody else and see qualities in that person that I don't have at all. It's helpful for me to think that whatever I see, I have the potential for. I may not display it much, but it's in there, and only because of that can I see it outside myself.

Cheri: Whatever you are seeing in someone else, you are seeing from your own experience. That's the critical point. They may be doing anything, or being anything, but what you see is part of you. How you label it, what you name it, how you describe it — that's you. What you experience around it is *your* experience.

Terry: It took me a long time to see that a projected quality can be one I resist. For instance, I could say, "John is loud," and I know I'm not loud, so I think I'm not projecting. It's easier to see the qualities I cling to; the things I push away are harder to recognize. But, in fact, being loud is an issue for me, because I don't allow myself to do it. It's just as much a part of me as something that I actively do.

Cheri: Yes. It's both sides of an issue.

Jeannie: Doesn't it also have to do with the values that you attach to "John is loud" — thinking loud is bad? Isn't judgment more the projection than just the plain fact? If you could simply say "John is loud," period, without anything else about it, then is that still projection, or is that just observation?

Cheri: Is there experience beyond projection? See if this is helpful. There is just the plain experience of something: the eyes are open, and the eyes see. But as soon as I turn it into an experience I am aware of, in that sense of knowing it or labelling it, I'm projecting. Every step of making experience into a "something" is through this filter. By the time I describe it, it's refiltered through concepts and language. At that point, it is very far from the original experience.

June: But isn't there some truth there, because we all agree on so much?

Cheri: What we have is a lot of common assumptions, postures, attitudes, beliefs. We don't often find ourselves in situations where there are people who have beliefs and assumptions that are very different from our own. When we are in that situation it's fascinating: we sit around saying things like, "In our culture we do so-and-so." It's like an interesting game we play, not paying attention to the fact that what we're saying is, "We make up our version of life this way. How do you make up yours?"

Also, we don't examine things very closely. We like to stick with broad statements, then we're comfortable because it feels like we're having the same experience as everybody else.

How much do we maintain that attitude of "I know what I should be, and I know that I am not that, and I can't seem to be that," because we are addicted to suffering, because we are comfortable with that conditioning? It gives us our identity, doesn't it? Because once we've turned away from our hearts, we are no longer identified with innocence, with our true nature. We have our identity in this illusion of separateness that comes about through socialization.

Until we get into something like this practice, it never occurs to us that those beginnings could be questioned. If we assume we are not equal to our circumstances, that we are fragile and confused, it's understandable that we go into each moment with a kind of "Oh-god-don't-get-me" posture. It would be difficult to imagine somebody just going in with their arms and their hearts and minds wide open, because, wouldn't a person assume they were going to get hurt? I mean, haven't we been? On enough occasions to pretty much guess that it would probably happen again. We could almost never assume that we could simply stop doing all the things we do to protect ourselves and that we would be all right.

But that's all there is to it. As soon as we drop all the ideas about who we are and what we must have to continue to be that—all the conditioned responses that lead us to abandon ourselves—as soon as we let that go, we're back to our true nature and we have everything we need.

❂

I'm Trying Really Hard
and It's Not Working

Any idea of wanting to make progress is already a regression . . .

Zen Master Bankei

Peter: My main stumbling block is the idea that there's another way that I could be, and then I wouldn't have to be doing spiritual practice. I could just do this other thing. And I'm an idiot for not doing it.

Cheri: Trying to change is what keeps us stuck. We are conditioned so heavily to try to improve ourselves, to change, to become a better person. When something happens that we don't like, instead of staying with it and seeing what's going on, we tend to leap into denial, fixing, apologizing, making it all right, covering it over, because we just had evidence that we're not the kind of person we should be — never noticing that that maintains being the very person that creates our problems.

Sylvia: That way, we never come to terms with whatever this "shouldn't be" is. And there's another approach: just saying, "Well, that's the way I am, what can I do? I'm trying."

Cheri: So you can go around this way, or you can go around that way. The only way that works is not going anywhere. Sitting still with yourself, just allowing whatever happens. Not taking it personally, not getting involved in it, not trying to push it away. Just paying attention. Then I begin to see what's going on — how I really am. Then judgment kicks in: "I shouldn't be that way, there's something wrong with me." So once again we are caught under that wheel of conditioned responses. And that's okay, because that's a part we've got to see — that being this way is just part of our whole response pattern.

Jeannie: What struck me when I first came to this practice from therapy was the idea that here you don't try to figure it out. In therapy, all that mental stuff goes on, and you think about it and look at it from every side, and that feels like you're doing something about it.

Sylvia: It reinforces the sense that "I'm trying."

Jeannie: Exactly. "I'm trying really hard and it isn't working. So it must be hopeless." So, I can stay who I am.

Cheri: My image is, your car is in the ditch, you're stuck. The wheel is spinning around, and you keep stepping on the accelerator because that feels like you're doing something. But you're just revving the engine and the wheel is spinning, and you're not going anywhere.

Jeannie: You're just digging yourself in deeper and deeper. And throwing mud around.

Cheri: Now what?

Sylvia: I accept that. Somehow when I fully accept it, then I'm not stuck anymore. I think that's what this process is all about — learning that acceptance. Only when you've fully accepted the situation can you see your options and act accordingly.

❁

How Change Happens

If you would clearly see the truth,
discard opinions pro and con.
To founder in dislike and like
is nothing but the mind's disease.
And not to see the Way's deep truth
disturbs the mind's essential peace.

Third Zen Patriarch Seng Tsan

Cheri: What do we mean by acceptance?

Jeannie: I think it's looking at whatever it is in ourselves and realizing what it comes from, that there's some need that caused it to arise, and so there's a purpose for its being there.

Cheri: Seeing it as an opportunity, not a punishment or a problem or a mistake.

Jeannie: And looking at it with compassion.

Cheri: But shouldn't you change it, no matter where it came from or why it's there or how much of an opportunity it is? Don't you have an obligation to get rid of it once you've understood all that?

Melinda: I think it changes itself.

Cheri: How does that happen?

Melinda: By not being struggled against. Without the resistance against it, it doesn't have any investment in keeping going.

Cheri: What is the payoff for resisting a part of yourself you don't like?

Sylvia: Being maintained. Staying yourself, your good old familiar self. Even if it's something you hate, it's part of your identity.

Greg: The idea that there is someone to change is where the problem is. All we have to do is leave things alone, and they'll change by themselves.

Peter: In reality we're *not* changing those things we see as bad. Intrinsically, we're good and whole and adequate, and all that's happening is we're letting go of *seeing* ourselves as being inadequate. Then everything is right there. By accepting it all, we are giving ourselves what we need.

Cheri: So, what we're seeking is what's there when we stop doing everything else. When we see clearly what we're doing and how we're doing it, in that moment of clarity, the maintenance system falls away, and we can see through to who we really are and what we're seeking.

What are some concrete examples? An example for me is, I don't like cilantro. And I dislike myself for that. I tell myself I should have no preferences, I should be beyond liking and disliking. Everything should taste exactly the same to me. Now, the moment I drop that — and it can be as simple as having an open, questioning mind about the assumption that a person has to like all foods equally, just opening up to the possibility that there's nothing wrong with not liking cilantro — suddenly everything is different, isn't it? I'm not such an awful person. It's all right to be this way.

Another issue: I'm a born nag. I used to think that was terrible, then I began to ask where the nagging was coming from; not, "This is a behavior I shouldn't have," but, "What's really going on with this?" And I saw that it came from love. That may not be obvious to everybody, but it was obvious to me. Nagging comes from wanting everybody to be all right, wanting them to be happy, to be careful and not hurt themselves or make mistakes or do something that's going to be upsetting to them. So, in seeing that there might be a good intention there, I can quit resisting and thereby maintaining it.

Also there's seeing that a behavior is simply not helpful, it's not accomplishing anything. Once we see that this behavior isn't getting me what I want, it automatically begins to fall away.

Jeannie: One situation in which it's especially clear that it doesn't work is trying to change another person. You see things that are wrong with another person, and you know how to fix them, so you set about telling them what's wrong and what they ought to do instead, and how they're kind of awful for doing it that way and you'd like them much better if they were this way. After awhile you see not only that it doesn't work, but it makes things worse.

Peter: It also makes whatever it is that you don't like in this person just that much stronger, because then they have to protect it against this attack.

Cheri: And this is how it works within ourselves, of course.

Bonnie: The funny thing is that we think we have a choice about accepting what we don't like. We think somehow by saying, "This is unacceptable," it's going to be different.

Sylvia: Acceptance has nothing to do with liking or disliking. It's a separate issue. So you can accept those things that aren't okay, you can accept not liking something. And accepting it allows you room to do something to change specific things in the situation. In fact, things may change just in and through that acceptance.

Cheri: How is accepting that I have a lousy marriage going to make it any better?

Greg: When you get out of the present, things get static. Such and such happened in the past, the future I envisioned isn't here, so the marriage is lousy. But if you stay in the present, the same thing is an ongoing process, and you can see it as, "I'm not happy with what's going on right now." And you might begin to think about what it is that you expect and how you got in this situation where you're feeling unhappy. Then it turns into something that moves, something with possibilities. But if you have "a lousy marriage," that's an idea that can't move — and you can maintain it and suffer with it for your whole life.

Cheri: It's external, it's this *thing,* this albatross, and there's nothing I can do about it because it's not me. What if I look instead to see how I maintain a situation?

Peter: If you're in the present, and you see what your marriage is in terms of how you are doing the marriage right this instant, that is a continuous thing which could be workable.

Cheri: Is that what we mean by it changes automatically — when we see it clearly for what it is, it becomes a different experience?

Terry: Yes. It's as if suddenly you go around the corner and everything's changed, and yet everything's the same. That's acceptance.

Cheri: In fact, sometimes it's changed so dramatically that we can't believe that nothing's changed. It's all the same people, and everybody's still themselves, but it looks so different . . .

Greg: I practice that when I'm suffering. I practice going back and forth between suffering and then shutting it off, just being aware of myself saying, "This is great," then being aware when I go back to, "This is terrible."

Also, there's the process of observing movement, sensation, feeling, thought, and action. I find that very useful in looking at experience, just like the concept of subpersonalities is useful. Especially because I can get lost in a lot of analyzing. But with smoking, for example, I just began to pay attention to that sequence, and I'd experience a sensation, then I'd want to smoke. You can experience the sensation, the thoughts, the feelings almost all at once, without thinking too much about it, and just let them go without worrying about where they come from.

Cheri: And with a little practice, you can just move from sensation to acceptance? Knowing that from that sensation will spring all these other things — and that's just how it is. If you can accept that, it can help you not repeat those laborious, unnecessary steps that often lead to more problems. Because when we start going through the thoughts about something and the emotional reaction to it and the action — remember, this is powerful conditioning! — it's easy to get about halfway through any one of those and get hooked right back in. And even as I say that, there's an awareness that not wanting to get hooked in is part of the problem.

Greg: Something happened to me a couple of days ago — I latched onto a fast train to hell. In a way, I didn't *want* to do it, but I did it anyway. It was as if there was someone within me who was suffering, and the way to find out all about that was to jump onto the train and go to hell with them and see if we could muddle our way back.

Cheri: In fact, the moment I think about where I am, where I'm going, where I should be, where I want to be, I'm already on my way to hell. The first thought of "me" and "I need to save me, I'm worried about me, something could happen to me, I've got to be careful of me" — big trouble.

Greg: Yeah. The other side of that is that cartoon at the Center with the guy in hell and he's pushing a wheelbarrow and whistling, and the caption reads, "Somehow we're not getting through to that guy."

Bonnie: There's another one I love, about our thinking we need to change. This person is looking at a sign that says, "You are here," and there's another sign saying, "You should be here."

Cheri: Actually, you probably would have reached a fair level of enlightenment if you could understand every cartoon on that bulletin board.

❁

Acceptance Versus Passivity

*All the effort must be made by you; Buddhas only show
the way.*

The Dhammapada

Bonnie: People who are not doing this practice often think
that letting go, or acceptance, is passive. But I see it as very
active.

Cheri: Yes, in contrast to avoidance. But how do you know
what is acceptance and what is resignation?

Sylvia: Resignation, to me, is a phony acceptance. It's saying
you accept it but still wishing it were otherwise.

Terry: In resignation, you're still suffering. And when you've
really accepted something, the suffering goes away.

Melinda: As long as you're holding out hope for the possibility
that it could be different, that's not acceptance.

Cheri: It's like the difference between letting go and giving up.
Giving up is what you do when you don't have a choice.

Greg: For me it's never that simple. Part of me can be resigned,
and all sorts of other things can be going on, including
acceptance. An example is that Jennifer [when she was work
coordinator at the monastery] tells me to do something, and
I just start doing it, then part of me says, "Why should she have
me do it and not Peter or somebody else?" So there are subpersonalities talking to me about this, and some are unhappy,
but I'm still there doing what she asked me to do, so there's
that level of acceptance. Resignation is more like hearing
yourself say, "This is terrible," and believing it. And feeling

like a hero when you make yourself go ahead and do it anyway.

Sylvia: I think that's a good point, because acceptance comes from the center, and it's not colored by an ego or subpersonality. You're not caught up in believing the subpersonality. If it's the subpersonality that's doing the accepting, it's probably more like resignation.

Cheri: When it comes from a centered place, there's probably very little to say about it. Even with something that was a big deal for you, if somebody mentions it, you might have a hard time getting back into your feelings about it because it's so completely finished for you. But with resignation, you'd probably be willing to go through the story forever.

Bonnie: It seems to me if something I've really accepted about myself comes up, it can be humorous, whereas before it never would have been.

Cheri: That's a good indication, yes. Also the level of tension around it. With resignation, whenever the subject comes up, you feel that tension.

Bhasa: It sounds like this discussion is implying that when we accept something, we don't have to change anything about it. That's something I had been confused about. But I just went through a situation a few weeks ago where it seemed like change was necessary. I realized that I had been in an abusive situation with a therapist and was deciding that I needed to do something about that. I went to Cheri and totally expected her to tell me to "just sit with it" and accept it. I was shocked that that was not her response. We didn't talk about acceptance very much; we talked about action and what my choices were. I felt like beating the therapist up, but my preconceived notion of Buddhism was that you just accept whatever's happening without trying to change anything. But in this situation, that was not appropriate. There are times when it's not okay to just sit with something.

Sylvia: It sounds to me as if the acceptance was in acknowledging the abusiveness of the situation. As long as you were denying it or saying, "Well, it's not really all that bad," or "There's something wrong with me," you were unable to do anything about it.

Bhasa: Yes, my acceptance led me to action.

Cheri: Because you were, in the moment of that acceptance, different. You were no longer a person who was willing to be in an abusive situation. So it had to change. You would have had to become passive to stay in that situation. Not be passive, but *become* passive. Because our normal approach to life is active. This happens, we do this in response; movement is constant. You would have had to say, "Now I'm *not* going to move" — in a very unnatural way — in order to stay where you were. I think that's what people are imagining with this idea of passivity. They think they would sit down and never move again. Of course that would be unnatural, and that's not at all what's suggested.

And, the other side of what's unnatural is elbowing our way through life. Making life happen. Pushing this way, pushing that, inflicting our will on everything. That's also unnatural. But we think of that as the way we should be, because we're so accustomed to it. We're socialized to believe that we have to take charge, make things happen, make decisions, approach life aggressively. And that's not true either.

The middle way is simply getting in sync with life, realizing that life "lives" you. That you are not separate from life. Whatever comes up in the moment, you rise to meet it, you are right there with it. Then your action is appropriate to life, because it is life.

So, either way of trying to separate yourself and get outside life — by not reacting or by trying to control — is going to be confusing or wrong. Not morally wrong, but it just doesn't feel right. It doesn't work.

But back to common misconceptions — this "just being in the present moment" and being responsible to yourself — where is the compassion? Doesn't this kind of attitude lead to other people not being in your universe? To separation?

Bhasa: No. I'll go back to this example that I brought up, because this was exactly my dilemma. I had already removed myself from getting hurt anymore, but the question was whether I was going to do something to prevent others in that situation from being harmed. Cheri's suggestion to me was to sit very quietly until I was clear about what I needed to do for myself. It took me a few weeks to come to a point of clarity about that, then I decided that what I needed did include taking action and responsibility for a larger community than just myself. Ultimately that was taking care of myself, because I couldn't live comfortably with myself knowing that other people who were in therapy with this person might be as vulnerable as I had been.

Cheri: That's the interesting part of it for me. When we are operating in the world, are we ever doing anything for anybody other than ourselves?

Bhasa: No.

❁

Embracing the One With the Problem

*. . . If we do not take refuge in the Buddha within ourselves,
there is no other place for us to retreat.*

Sixth Zen Patriarch Hui-neng

Sylvia: I have found a way of paying attention that allows a subpersonality to just be there in unconditional love and acceptance. You know how subpersonalities come in pairs — one appears, then another one comes around to take care of the first one. This happens in a way that is very cyclical and repetitive, so it can seem hopeless. But I have learned that in allowing one subpersonality to be there in full acceptance, a certain disidentification happens and another subpersonality doesn't have to come to the rescue.

Cheri: And that automatically breaks the cycle?

Sylvia: Yes. Instead of getting caught up with this second subpersonality who just makes it worse — arguing or denying or becoming defensive or blaming someone else to protect the first one — there's this sense of not just watching, but being with that part of yourself, being it.

Cheri: Allowing, and yet disidentified. It's like sitting with a friend who's really sad or upset and just allowing that person to express that in whatever way is required.

Sylvia: But there isn't necessarily anything to be done about it.

Jeannie: And that lets you feel compassion for whatever it is that's suffering, instead of being angry with it or rationalizing with it or all the other things . . .

Cheri: . . . that we do to try to get rid of it. Let's work through this with an addictive behavior. There's the part of me, say, who wants to eat all the time. She doesn't care if she weighs five hundred pounds. There's another part of me who's terrified of her, who not only doesn't want this one to eat, but actively wants to be thin, healthy, and all that sort of thing. What do I do? If I give in to the one who wants to eat, she's going to weigh five hundred pounds — and so will I. So, how can I allow her to be?

Terry: Find out what the food represents, ask what she really wants. This is not true physical hunger.

Cheri: But what if she won't tell me what she really wants? And I'm already up to three hundred pounds?

Peter: Give her unconditional love and whatever it is she says she wants.

Cheri: Even if I gain a few pounds, I can risk it?

Sylvia: It might be worse to allow the one who wants to be skinny to control the situation. That's what I was talking about — the one who comes along to fix up the first one may cause more trouble. That's how we usually take care of ourselves. We have some tendency we don't like, so we take care of it by creating its opposite. And it's very important that the one I prefer stay in control.

June: So we might live our life with the skinny one in control, but the issue never gets resolved. There is this unending struggle.

Bonnie: When you step back from it, you can see these subpersonalities in action. There's a part of me that's hopeless and overwhelmed, and I have this other part that's strong and independent and doesn't want any help. The first one starts in with, "I'm so helpless, I need help." But when somebody tries to help me, the other one says, "Hey, I don't need any help, I'm fine, back off." This happened with someone I really care about, and as a result, things began going terribly wrong. When I finally saw the connection between the two subpersonalities and how they operated, it didn't happen anymore.

Cheri: You don't even have to try not to do it any longer. You just can't do it in the same way. Now, the not-so-good news is, that may not happen with one shot.

Bonnie: For me, it's a cue. When one of these two starts, it catches my attention.

Cheri: And you know that paying attention to it and seeing it clearly is what's going to resolve it. Not choosing which part of you is the best and pushing the other one away. That doesn't work, and we know it because we've been trying to do that all our lives. It's taking care of both of them that begins to end the whole drama.

Jeannie: But it doesn't work to say, "Okay, now I have to give this obnoxious part of me unconditional love and acceptance." Just saying it does no good.

Bhasa: When I have trouble with that, I take the idea of embracing and exaggerate it. A part of me who shows up a lot is a little victim. I picture her in my mind's eye and pull her to me and hold her, until she's through with what she's feeling, which is persecution. And I know that right behind her will be the judge, waiting to criticize the victim for being that way. So I say, "Judge, come out now — you get your hug, too." When I can stay in that place, it changes the whole picture, and everybody seems happy.

Cheri: In looking at aspects of ourselves — as with anything in life — we usually assume that the one who's being pointed at is the one with the problem. But look for the one that's identifying something as a problem — that's the one who has the problem. Start there: see who has the problem and take care of that one. Then see who's behind that one, and take care of that one. Because when you take care of the one with the problem, someone else will usually emerge immediately to fill that opening.

Jeannie: To me it feels condescending to try to hug those mad little subpersonalities, as if I'm saying, "Now, come on, calm down, and let yourself be hugged." There's something awful about that.

Peter: It seems extra, this other part of me who is trying to talk in a way that isn't natural or how I would normally do it. The one who's saying, "Come here, let me hug you," simply because I've heard about approaching subpersonalities that way . . .

Cheri: I would want to know who is this "I" that is doing this? It doesn't feel like it's coming from a very centered place.

Melinda: It sounds like it's shifting to a person who says there's no reason to be upset, which is sort of . . .

Sylvia: . . . like *trying* to do the process instead of doing it.

Cheri: I suspect it's pseudo-Zen. Pseudo-Zen is a subpersonality that is slightly off center and who says things like, "I am your centered self, I'll take care of this." And says terribly wise things like, "Oh, well, it doesn't matter anyway."

Peter: Or, "That's life."

Jeannie: Who tries to say all the right things. Who takes all the stuff we learn here and remembers little lines like, "Come here and let me hug you."

June: You don't have to do something that seems false to you. You can simply allow a subpersonality to be, just by not turning away from that part of yourself.

Jean: I've found that I can be compassionate in allowing a part of myself to not want to be hugged and loved. Thinking "I've got to hug, I've got to love, I've got to embrace" is getting right back into the bondage.

Sylvia: I like the image of the wild animal, or maybe a small child. It doesn't want to be hugged, but if you just sit there patiently with it . . .

Cheri: It'll be in your lap.

Melinda: We assume sometimes that hugging is what that part of us might want, but it's important to find out — to just sit with that part and ask what it needs.

Cheri: Yes. This is part of the process of "looking." Asking a part of ourselves, what do you want, what do you need, what's your world look like? Why do you want it to be different? Those kinds of getting-to-know-you questions.

Jean: If you're just plain loved as you grow up, hugging and so on is fine. But there can be a lot of pain along with love. What might be going on with some of us who don't want to be hugged and loved is that there's too much pain there.

Cheri: Yes. Some aspects of ourselves have been hurt, and they are not very trusting. It is important to allow that untrusting part to experience whatever it's experiencing.

Greg: That's important for me, because I never—well, it seems we're getting carried away about hugging subpersonalities. A lot of people talk about it that way, but I just never have. What's helpful for me is a simple recognition, "Ah, there's somebody," and just, "Howdy," and that's it. Just letting it be, just being together in the same space. I never have any confidence in the one who is doing the talking, doing the recognizing, and so on. So my experience with subpersonalities is just of this bunch of us here, sharing the space.

Cheri: And that experience must be coming from a fairly centered place, because everybody is feeling basically all right?

Greg: Yes. But if I start being too active in it, it's generally not coming from a centered place.

Peter: When I try embracing and even addressing questions to subpersonalities, it comes from a sincere effort, but it seems fake. Especially when I am angry, the last thing I want is to have anybody embrace me.

Cheri: These are just techniques that point in the direction of loving, accepting attention. It doesn't matter how you describe it once you know how to be right there with these parts of yourself and let them know they are perfectly fine just as they are. Sometimes it helps to talk about it in these terms that are familiar to us from our relationships with people outside ourselves. It may be easier to see it if we say we all know that when you're around somebody who is sensitive to you, who listens to you, who obviously cares what your experience is, there is a tendency to trust more, to be willing to open up. If you're approaching those parts of yourself in that way, over a period of time, they're going to think, "Hey, I think he's seen the light, I think he genuinely cares." Then there's more of a willingness to open up and trust you — a more centered you — to be the person they deal with. But all you have to do is be fully present, however you do that.

Jeannie: That takes the pressure away from having to perform or say anything.

Peter: So you don't have to be there saying, "Now I am paying attention to you, now I'm loving you"?

Cheri: Not at all. The process is almost like getting out of the way so they can finally just be who they are. Then it's fascinating, because you can be sitting there getting to know yourself for the first time, without judgment creating that distance. I love that part.

Jeannie: But I'm thinking about that person who's going to weigh five hundred pounds pretty soon, and balancing out the being with that person and accepting what that person wants and so on, and at the same time not allowing that person's destructive behavior. . .

Cheri: Not believing it. Not believing her conditioned responses.

Jeannie: She says, "I want this more than anything else." And you say, "I know."

Cheri: And when you really do know that, and where it's coming from, which is that life is tough . . . .
We're conditioned to want all these things. We're miserable because the very things we are addicted to and crave don't make us happy, but not having them certainly is no thrill either.

So there you are with the part of yourself who overeats. It's hard to just sit there with her through all that — and that's what you do. You don't have to be confused, and you don't have to support her confusion in thinking that going to the refrigerator is going to help. You know it is not the answer, and even she doesn't believe it anymore. When she finally lets that go, it's actually a relief. Not that she doesn't feel despair when she gives up her one crutch, her one hope that there was a way out of this: that's a very low point, and it's good if somebody can be there with her then, just being there in total acceptance of it all.

But in that moment of letting go, we're suddenly able to see what the alternatives really are — to see where real freedom is. To discover real comfort. Real joy. Deep gratitude.

❂

TAKING REFUGE
IN THE PRACTICE:
MONKS

In 1986 the Center purchased three hundred and twenty acres of rolling foothills in Calaveras County to use as a retreat center. One-room hermitages were built from scrap materials; scattered at some distance from each other among the manzanita, oaks, and pines, they provide accommodation for people living there and some of the retreatants and guests (others camp). For several years, cooking and eating facilities were housed in one large tent, the meditation hall in an adjacent one — appropriately labeled, courtesy of the Army Medical Corps, MED TENT. Kerosene lanterns provided light, propane fueled the kitchen appliances, a generator provided electricity for power tools, and water was carried from a nearby well in gallon containers. With the addition of a solar-heated shower, a temporary meditation hall, and an organic garden and orchard, civilization seemed imminent. By 1990, there was running water and solar electricity, and construction began on a rammed-earth building that will include kitchen and dining room, common room and workshop, and dormitory. Rammed earth, which uses soil from the building site mixed with small amounts of sand and cement, is not only ecologically superior to most contemporary construction methods, but, being highly labor-intensive, is well suited to certain intangible purposes of a monastery.

In Buddhism, monastic training does not require irrevocable vows or lifelong commitment; rather it is a period, of any length, during which a student agrees to observe strict guidelines, such as silence, and to work closely with a teacher, which may mean doing what you are told rather than what you would like. In addition to meditation and spiritual direction, monastic life typically entails long hours of hard work under difficult conditions. Such a situation offers many occasions for resistance—egocentricity asserting its sovereignty—and thus provides abundant opportunities for seeing exactly how suffering comes about.

In February 1990, I conducted group interviews with the six people living on the land as monks. We gathered in the meditation hall, a low, screened building set among live oaks at the edge of a meadow. Greg, Phyllis, and Jennifer have been at the monastery since the beginning; Diane and Cameron had come for several months; and Terry had been there only a few weeks. Before coming here to live, they had worked as a graphic designer, an advertising executive, a computer hardware analyst, a training manager for a computer company, and two Montessori teachers; Phyllis is also a Roman Catholic nun who has permission from her order to follow Buddhist practice as well as Catholicism (she attends mass in a nearby town). Cheri, the teacher, was present the first day, as was Greg's dog Murphy. On the second day, Cheri was not there, and Murphy's place was taken by Phyllis's dog Bo, an ancient part-Pomeranian wearing a green sweater.

Among the monks, Cheri is most often referred to as the "guide." She describes her role in this way to indicate that she is simply traveling the path ahead of us and can offer directions based on her experience. The term also reminds us that the source of the teaching is not the individual named Cheri. The guidance comes from within; we may hear it first in the teacher's voice, but her work is to help us find for ourselves that "True Nature" of unconditional love. Thus, we began with questions about the teacher-student relationship.

How do you work with a teacher? What is the role of a teacher in a student's life? (Dispensing information seems the least of it: what is the deeper process?) Why do you need a teacher? How is the teacher — or teaching — internalized as you look inward to find your own guidance? And how, as students, do you grow into being teachers yourselves?

The monks' responses to these and other questions are often very funny, and when I think of their faces, I see them smiling and laughing. There is no trace of the dourness or deprivation often associated with monastic training; on the contrary, it would be difficult to find six people more vitally, intensely, happily involved in life. They remind me of a statement made by Leon Bloy that Cheri posted at the Zen Center: "Joy is the most infallible sign of the presence of God."

✪

Working With the Teacher

Train your eyes and ears; train your nose and tongue. The senses are good friends when they are trained. Train your body in deeds, train your tongue in words, train your mind in thoughts. This training will take you beyond sorrow.

The Dhammapada

Jennifer: Before I came to this practice, I was doing a lot of searching. It felt like I was banging my head against different walls, not being able to figure out what I wanted, what I was looking for. When I came to the Zen Center, I felt a connection between what I saw in the guide and what I wanted to find in myself. I had had some introduction to Zen before that and had developed a sitting practice, but I didn't have much understanding of Zen from reading. I sensed that I needed somebody to help me focus on this nebulous thing I was looking for.

Recently it's become clear to me that having a teacher represents following my heart. When I'm following the teacher's guidance, it looks like I'm following something external to myself—and it has to look like that for me, because that's how I let go of ego. When I follow something externally, my ego isn't leading me right then. That's how I've learned to come back and follow my heart.

Following my heart means being open to everyone and everything. Including the ego. I don't know if it's possible to do that without a teacher. For me, it didn't seem to be. The teacher guides me to places I wouldn't go by myself.

Terry: For me, it seems that the guide has been to a place that I have forgotten. There's some remembrance of it inside me, but I've forgotten the details of how to get there. And that's what touched me, that here's a person who's clearly been where I need to go, and if I follow this person, she can guide me until I am able to guide myself — until my whole being remembers what it is that I've forgotten.

Cameron: I'm sort of new to Zen and to this group. Before coming here I used to go once a week after work to meditation and group discussion, and that was my Zen practice. Then I gradually came more often to retreats here and to workshops and discovered that each time, something was awakened in me that is bigger than my intellect and my ego, and I grew immeasurably. Finally I felt that I wanted to do this all the time.

Sara: Is there something different about the way you work with the teacher once you've committed to monastic life?

Cameron: I'm finding I don't know much about what it means to follow the teacher. My ego flails against being in a student–teacher relationship, so I'm struggling with that. And it's interesting to watch, because I didn't know much about my ego. I keep coming around to that same conflict, but each time it's on a different level, and each time I find that something other than my ego has grown and opened in understanding.

Terry: I had been in guidance with the teacher once a week for the last several years, and doing two group discussions a week and going to as many workshops and retreats as I could. But I got to a point where I knew that if I was going to do this spiritual training, and if it meant as much to me as I said it did, I had to live it instead of just talking about it. And coming here meant living it.

As for my relationship with the guide, my perception is that it has changed dramatically. Once I got here, it seemed that she and I had this agreement that she is not only the heart I follow, she's also life. She's everything I come up against that's hard. The unspoken agreement is that she will put before me all the hard stuff. That's how it's changed.

Phyllis: I will always be eternally grateful that I found this particular teacher and ended up in this particular place. I can't seem to do what I know is in me to do without a lot of pushing and prodding.

I've noticed all along that there is some kind of guidance inside of me. Some of the time I'll see a direction I need to be taking in my life — it's like getting clues — and then that's the very direction I start getting from the guide. I used to think, "Gosh, she's magic," but then I realized that I had seen it first. That's made me realize that if we pay good enough attention, we can be more our own teacher. At some point, everything becomes the teacher; everything you look at, everything you encounter is something to learn from.

But I'm certainly not ready to give up the guide — no way. Because she's leading me where my heart wants to go. Even if I get a glimpse of it myself, I'm still too timid, there are too many conditions — all the stuff that keeps us from our true nature.

Terry: Someone asked me recently, "How could you go off to live in a place with someone telling you what to do twenty-four hours a day?" And, I do hate that. One of my biggest issues is that I hate being told what to do. Which is why I'm here.

And here the guide represents life. Every moment I'm alive, life is telling me what to do. At first, of course, it scared me. But what seems to be happening is that the guide mirrors for me all the hard things I come up against in life. By giving up control to someone, I'm asking to be given that experience. There's nowhere I can go, I can't hide, I can't fight it, so let's see what happens.

To do that, there has to be faith not only in the teacher, but in myself. I recognize that this is what's necessary, and that the capability is there to — I started to say "do" it, but it's not doing, it's *being* with what's happening. I know that what I'm practicing over and over is developing something in me that I couldn't do on my own. Out there in the world, if life presented me with a situation that was just too scary, I would usually run away. But here I have to stay with it, be with it, watch what I do with it. That for me is the value of being in this place and working with the guide.

Diane: For me it's been a long, slow, cautious process. I've probably been working with the guide longer than anyone here, possibly twice as long. But I've only been here at the monastery for six weeks. I've been very resistant to finally just stepping into it. It took a long time to get here.

The guide said to me years ago that you'll come to realize that the thing you think is your greatest asset is actually your biggest obstacle. I've always thought my greatest asset was my mind. And that has clearly gotten in my way. But I have finally gotten to a point where it's clear that this is where I need to be. It feels in the last six weeks that once the resistance was gone, once my mind wasn't in the way anymore, everything — I finally just let go, allowed life to happen.

And it's like a waterfall. What the guide is doing is — I would have to say she is getting out of the way, too. She's just listening to the cascade.

I haven't seen a big difference in our relationship since I came here. But this other process is going on, and a lot of what happened between us for the first ten years isn't there anymore, because everything is just happening inside me, on its own.

Of course there is still resistance. "I don't want to be here, it's cold, it's primitive . . ." But that's secondary to all the wonderful things that are going on.

Greg: Accepting a teacher, a guide, has been the most important step I've taken in spiritual training. For several years before I started practicing at our Center, I came into contact with several people who might have been good spiritual guides, but I wasn't willing to accept them in that role. I did some shopping around to find a "good" teacher, which I guess meant someone who was "good enough for me." It took a year of attempting Zen practice for me to realize that I needed to do something differently — to take the leap of faith of accepting another person as a teacher.

At the time all I actually knew was that despite all my efforts to become a better person, to be happy, I was not a better person or happy. Our teacher did seem happy, and I concluded that she must know what I wanted to know. At this stage she represented the solution to my problems. I felt that if I could be like her, I could be happy too.

Accepting the teacher as the solution to my problem had two sides. One was the pure aspect of "buddha recognizing buddha," that is, coming into contact with a part of me that knew that suffering is not inevitable, that enlightenment exists. The other was the not-so-pure aspect of "egocentricity recognizing buddha," or "I'm going to figure out how to get enlightened from her."

Buddha recognizing buddha is what has really sustained me in the practice. Egocentricity recognizing buddha is what led me into the second phase of my relationship with our teacher, which is the teacher as my big problem. I spent a long time trying to figure out how to coax her into giving me enlightenment, primarily through trying to show her how deserving I was — by demonstrating how good, talented, and smart I was and other people weren't. This didn't work. When my ego tried to get enlightened, she would enthusiastically shout something like, "Whenever you think you're right, you're wrong!" (Buddhist teachers don't get angry, they get enthusiastic.)

I've matured a little in the practice. This means that sometimes the teacher looks like the solution to my problem, sometimes she looks like my problem, and sometimes our relationship is altogether different. This altogether different aspect is hard to describe because in a way it's sort of mystical and miraculous, and in a way it's very ordinary. It's what we call being centered, or being at one with all that is, or being in the present moment. When I'm centered, I meet the guide where she lives. She doesn't have to be physically present, and in a way it has nothing to do with her — because if I'm centered, everything is the teacher. Still, I feel that whenever I think of "my teacher," I will think of her. I'm very grateful to have met her.

A Zen teacher doesn't give a student anything but acceptance. She accepts the student, just as he is. Sometimes the acceptance feels warm and cozy; sometimes it seems hot and angry, or cold and aloof; sometimes it feels like nothing at all. This acceptance of the student is acceptance of what is — being in the moment. So really the only thing the teacher does is Zen practice. She embodies the practice, and if circumstances are right, the student will follow her example and begin to embody the practice also. I always had the impression of other teachers that they were enlightened, which meant that they didn't have to do anything anymore. That may not be true, but it was my impression. And what strikes me about our teacher is that she keeps on doing the practice. It's clear that she's doing what we're learning to do. So when I look at her as an example, it's never anymore as a perfect being, but as far as I can tell, as someone who does this practice all the time.

Another role she's played for me, whether she intended it or not, is keeping me from settling for anything less than the highest aspiration. I don't want to call it "my" highest aspiration, so I'll say whatever it was that got me to start this practice — it seemed very pure. But there's a tendency to settle for less than that, to turn it into something comfortable and easy, as if I've gone far enough. When I do that, the teacher turns me back to that pure aspiration. I keep getting through layers and layers, and reaching points where things are pretty much the way I like them. Then I want to keep it just like it is and have everything be certain and me be just kind of moderately enlightened. But that always gets pointed out to me, and my relationship with the teacher keeps me on track, because it won't settle for less.

❂

How We Got Here

> . . . *Straight ahead runs the Way.*
> *Our form now being no-form,*
> *in going and returning we never leave home.*
> *Our thought now being no-thought,*
> *our dancing and songs are the voice of the dharma.*

> *Zen Master Hakuin*

Sara: You didn't come here simply to learn Buddhism . . .

Terry: No. I don't know much about Buddhism. I am here because I had been searching for something all my life. I didn't think it was a religion, but when I heard what was being taught at the Zen Center, my heart said, "This is it."

Sara: The others of you, what drew you here originally?

Phyllis: The guide gave a workshop in the community where I was living. I didn't know at that point that she was coming from a Buddhist background. But some of the words and phrases she used struck so true with parts of me, and with the spiritual practice I'd done for so long. One workshop led to another, and we eventually built the Zen Center.

It seemed to me that when we would get to a certain point, what she was teaching would change a little bit — she would make it more spiritual, more religious, you know. [Laughter] Then some people would drop away. But some of us stayed, and the teaching would move to another level, and it just kept on like that until it is what it is today. Which is — constantly changing.

Then we wanted a place for a retreat center and monastic training. This was what I'd always wanted, the more contemplative type of life. I knew it was going to be a lot of work, but I'd always had this other fantasy of being a farmer, an outdoors person. This seemed like the perfect opportunity for both.

Still, our life here changed and changed and changed, like a living organism, a thing in its own right. For me, it is very different now from the way it was when I first got involved.

I can't see at this point how I can live without this practice, certainly without this intense kind of spiritual training. Although it wouldn't necessarily have to be here, or this particular kind of environment or whatever, because — who knows what life holds?

For me, being a religious fanatic anyhow, I like that it's a religion, I like the Buddhism part. That makes it really wonderful, really rich. Personal growth — a lot of people do that, but the whole spiritual dimension is where it all meshes together, and to hear the wisdom of the Buddhist tradition, along with my own Christian tradition — it's overwhelming to me, I just love it.

Terry: Me, too, and I'm surprised at that. Sometimes I sit in my hermitage at night, and I think, "I'm a Buddhist monk. How did this happen?" Four years ago I certainly wouldn't have said that I was going to be a religious person, but now it feels like a devotion and a commitment. For the first time in my life, I'm connected to my heart in a way that I have never been connected to anything. To be committed on that deep a level to something that's bigger than anything I ever thought I was, which doesn't depend on any externals — and it's this ancient religion! — that's pretty miraculous.

Diane: I was watching an incredibly beautiful sunset the other night, and I was struck by the thought, "How did I get here?" Because the decision that made me come here didn't have anything to do with monastic training. It had to do with running away. Once I had made the commitment and told everybody that this was what I was going to do, I was stuck. There was no way out.

One of the things I was running away from was a long history of half-participation in life. Suddenly I found myself in a monastery, and it's very difficult to half-participate here. I am still dealing with the same subpersonality who wants to leave and has left retreats early any number of times, but I'm so grateful that I'm here, having this clear look at that part of myself. So it feels as if I came here through the back door. I never meant to do this, but it's where I need to be, and now there's no escape.

Cheri: The voice ringing in my ears right now is Cameron's saying, "What is this Buddhist monk stuff? I never said I wanted to be a Buddhist monk!"

Phyllis: That did kind of get slipped in on all of us.

Greg: Except for me. I wanted to be a Buddhist monk. In fact, maybe this is just my perception, but I think I kind of pushed us into this.

Cheri: You definitely wanted to be a monk. "When do I get to shave my head? What do I put down for 'occupation' when I fill out forms?"

Sara: Why did you want to become a Buddhist monk?

Greg: Whatever it is that causes us to do this, the longing to be home, to be free — that's what started me out. After awhile, it turned into wanting to be special, but it started out — I don't know. I was tired of what I was doing, finished with it — none of that stuff worked anymore. I had an experience where it became clear that being a monk was what I was to do, and that was when I started harassing the guide about it.

I didn't know exactly what it would mean. I thought it might mean that you would automatically wake up — at least being a monk would help a lot. [Laughter] Well, there's a way that that's so, but it wasn't the way I thought it was.

It took awhile to pay all the bills and get free of my job and stuff. Then I started doing the Carmel retreat schedule on my own, showing up at the Zen Center every day and doing work (I lived around the block). One day during the rest period of the Carmel schedule, I took a nap for the first time. And the guide telephoned me and said, "Where are you? What are you doing?" I said I was taking a nap. The next day she gave me this schedule that was rougher than the Carmel schedule.

I had made arrangements with a friend to go to Yosemite for one last fling before — I knew not what. So I brought my calendar to the guide and explained how I was going to do this one little thing, going to Yosemite, and she said, "That's not in keeping with the training of a monk." And I was just blasted away. Somehow, though, it became very clear that that was true, and that training as a monk was what I wanted.

What that means to me has changed a lot in the last couple of years, and the only way to describe it is that I want to do this practice more than anything. It changes its form, it's been changing ever since I've been here, and I expect it will keep changing. But the thing that's still true is that I just want to do what we're doing here. I always wanted to do this, it's just that all the ideas I had about what it meant were pretty goofy. And not true. And probably necessary.

Terry: That was true for me too. I quit my job knowing that part of my life just didn't work, and I didn't want to do it anymore. At that point I hadn't decided to come here. I said to myself, "I really want to follow my heart. And I don't know what's going to happen." It wasn't even a decision. Within a month it seemed obvious that I had quit my job because something inside me knew that I was preparing to come here. There was nothing else out there in the world that I wanted to do more than this.

I had all these ideas about what it might be. Parts of me were disappointed when I got here, and other parts of me said, "Yes, of course this is what it is."

This was what I had been searching for all my life without knowing it. I always knew that something very unusual and very big was going to happen — not something I was going to do, but something I would be involved in — and I didn't know what it was until last year, when it became so clear that this is it. When I saw that — not in my head, but in my heart — when I quit my job and had nothing to go to, no livelihood, only enough money for a matter of months, there was this faith inside that said, just do it: in order for you to know what's next, you have to make a space. This was the thing I had waited for all my life.

Cheri: It's so interesting to me to hear you say that, because that has been my experience for as long as I can remember. And the words that would go through my mind were, something wonderful is going to happen to me. I knew it wasn't that I was going to marry Prince Charming; I knew it wasn't ordinary. It was something — wonderful. When I found this practice, I knew this was it.

Greg: Did it take you awhile to figure it out?

Cheri: No. For me, it happened when I found my teacher. After I spent the first afternoon with him at the monastery, I said, "I'm home. This is it. This is what I've been waiting for all of my life."

Terry: When I first walked into the Zen Center, when I first heard you speak, that's exactly what went through my mind as I sat there. In my heart I felt, "These are the words I've heard inside myself all of my life. For the first time, I feel like I'm home." I had never felt at home anywhere. Once that connection was made, there was no more deciding to be done. I just kept going, and the next thing was the next thing. There were no more choices. So that's why I sit there at night and wonder how this happened. Because I didn't make it happen. I can't even tell you what the steps were, really, that got me here. But something inside me knew that this was the path.

Sara: I want to hear why Cameron came here. If it wasn't to be a Zen monk, what was it?

Cameron: First of all, when I decided to come here it was still called a retreat center, and after I came it started being called a monastery. So I came thinking I was going to be doing intensive spiritual training, but assuming that would be like an extended retreat. And to get here and find out suddenly it's a monastery and I'm being referred to as a monk — I hadn't agreed to all that. So only now that I'm here am I learning what monastic training is.

On retreats I felt connected with something very true, with parts of myself that I wanted to know more about. So I came out of faith in the teacher and confidence that I would be guided through the process of discovering what this was all about.

I established a commitment with myself that I would be here for six months, with no expectation that after that I would have to leave and do something else or that I'd be a failure if I didn't stay. I just wanted to leave it completely open to allow six months out of my life for intensive spiritual development, to be open to whatever that brought me and wherever that led me, without a preconceived notion of where I would be at the end of that time. I think it's the first time I've ever just followed my heart, just said, let's go.

I made an attempt to quit my job. When I went in to resign, and they asked how long I was going to be doing this, I said six months, and they offered me a leave of absence. So

I accepted it because it extended my insurance. And I sublet my apartment instead of giving it up. So, all the decisions I labored so hard over in order to allow myself to come here, all those decisions still have to be made. They'll still be waiting for me.

Somebody asked me a few weeks ago where I pictured myself in six months. I was surprised that I have no picture at all. And surprised that it didn't bother me that I didn't have a picture.

Phyllis: I never made a conscious decision to come. We started the process of looking for a place for a retreat center, and all along I just knew I would be here. There was no "Let's see, shall I quit my job? What are the pros and cons?" — none of that. Finally, the questions came up, "Well, if we did have a retreat center, would anybody go live there?" And I raised my hand.

Even with all my other spiritual training, I knew that somewhere, somehow, there would be a place or a time where someone would teach me to do what I was always saying I wanted to do. It just never happened before. On some level, I knew that this was what it was going to be, this was going to be the place. I never once made any choice for it, and never once doubted this choiceless choice.

❂

Daily Practice in Monastic Life

It is through the daily actions of our body and mind . . . that
we directly become enlightened . . . . There is no need to
change our existing body and mind, for the direct realization
of the Way. . . is neither to be bound by old viewpoints nor to
create new ones; it is simply to realize the Way.

Zen Master Dogen

Sara: I wonder if some of you would be willing to talk about specific incidents in which you were presented with a challenge by the teacher — what you went through, and where you came out on the other side.

Jennifer: I was thinking about that when I walked up to the kitchen to turn the oven on for lunch. Before I started this practice, I had this idea that there were certain things I knew how to do. I had pretty much established what they were and was comfortable within that; I made my life within the framework of things I was good at. After I moved here, I was asked to do things I didn't know how to do. Cooking, or planting fruit trees, or bookkeeping. The part of me that thinks it knows things has no interest in those things at all, because it doesn't know how to do them. But the requirement here is to make a shift, to be willing to take on new jobs, and in doing so, to go through a process of "I don't know how, it's scary," to the real nitty-gritty stuff, which is really, "I don't want to."

At all points during that process, there is support for continuing to look at your reactions. None of those feelings is a reason to stop. There's continually having to move from "I don't know," and wanting to stop there, to an open place of not knowing. Not moving into knowing, but moving through the anxiety and the illusion that there is something to know, letting go the idea of an end point where I can feel, "Good, now I'm a cook," or, "Now I'm a gardener and that's all over." The process is one of constantly staying with not knowing and still — every day, it seems like — doing new things, doing the specific tasks you think you don't know how to do.

Phyllis: One of the biggest challenges for me was putting aside the image of who I am — stopping to look at who I called myself, who I thought I was, all my postures about that, and start looking and accepting the real self, the real person. I remember two or three months of intense looking that was very hard because I wasn't accepting. Then when I was finally able to accept all the stuff I didn't want to see — at that point it felt like I could start doing this practice. After that I could see what I had to work with, and then when I would paint one of these images of myself, I could see through it pretty easily.

Sara: What were some of the steps involved in becoming able to look at an image of yourself and then let go of it?

Phyllis: A lot of it was subpersonality work, looking and accepting the subpersonalities that were there. A lot of it was projection, having the guide point out that what I see out there is what is in here.

Cheri: In other words, you would be having trouble with one of the other people who lived here, one of the other monks, and you would be encouraged to own that as a projection of yourself.

Phyllis: Yes, that's one way it would work. And also a lot of my work was with seeing how I did and said things because I thought I should — I should be good, I should live this way, I should be a saint. The guide would say, instead of "should be good," just "be good." There was that shift . . .

Cheri: It was from the heart, then, not from the ego.

121

Greg: From the ego, it's like this: if I know I should be good, that's a little bit superior to people who obviously don't know they should be good, otherwise they'd act differently. So even if I'm not good, at least I know I "should" be.

Phyllis: The guide would keep saying that with all this suffering, one learns humility and compassion for others. And you wouldn't want to end up being enlightened without humility and compassion. So to get off my high horse, which one of my subpersonalities was on . . .

Greg: So that's what I saw in the road!

Phyllis: My horse?

Cheri: I think he's referring to the signs of a high horse having passed by . . .

Phyllis: That was our cow. [Laughter] Anyway, the shift was just to let go all these images and move into reality, step out into the universe and be all that instead.

Cameron: I'm learning that there's an unconscious hook in thinking that if I'm good, I'm going to get something back. It's kind of an ugly good, there's a twinge of not-so-good in it. I see that sometimes when I get my feelings hurt, it's because I thought I was doing all this good stuff and I should reap the benefits. Whereas true goodness is for its own sake, not because something will come from it later on.

Diane: I've realized that when I do a good thing, I expected the goodness to last for awhile. There comes to mind a cartoon I'll bet every one of us has posted on our refrigerator doors. It's by Gahan Wilson and shows two Zen monks sitting, and the old one says to the younger one, "Nothing comes next. This is it."

And I'm realizing that there is nothing next, that you've got to keep doing it, that bliss doesn't last. Next moment, it all changes. You have to keep doing the good thing, or at least get out of the way and let it happen.

Greg: One example I remember of getting something cleared up was when I was upset about the way people here treated tools. To me it was obvious, here we are at this spiritual training center, we're supposed to be mindful, everyone knows you're supposed to take good care of tools, you shouldn't mistreat them or break anything or lose anything and so on —

Cameron: Isn't that right?

Greg: Yes, it is! [Laughter] But the point of this discussion is, I had this spading fork I was very fond of, and there was someone here who, I was sure, was going to mess it up. So I thought that before he used it, I would teach him how to use it properly. He told the guide about this, and I got a note from her saying that any tool that had anything to do with me was to be collected and put away and never used here again. Of course I was upset and afraid, and I talked to the guide about it. I just kept telling her how awful this was, that things would get broken and people didn't know how to treat them. She said that people were here to learn about other things, and that the tools weren't so important, and we had to go through quite a long time of breaking down this notion I had about the sacredness of tools.

Finally I said, "I'm trying to protect *myself.*" And she said, "Now, that's something we can work with."

For me the connection was, if people don't take care of tools, it's as if they're abusing me. By going through all my reactions about this, I finally got to that connection. So now, when this comes up (and it comes up all the time), I pay attention to the sensations, feelings, and thoughts that always go on in this situation and realize that someone in me feels abused. But not by whoever's using the tools — it isn't their responsibility—it's going on within me. This interaction with the teacher made me come up against that. Now I know when that process starts, when I grumble about somebody in my head, then I have that incident to remember, and the grumbling is a reflection of something else, something I can work with, which is in me.

Terry: When I first got here, the way we do clean-up after meals felt like an assault. I'm used to living alone and eating alone and doing things a certain way, and here it felt like chaos. I thought everyone should be assigned a job — Jen wash the dishes, Terry sweep the floor, Greg do this — so I could know what to expect, so I could feel safe. It's that person in me who wants to know everything that's going to happen. I struggled with that simple thing for a long time. It felt just awful.

Now clean-up is kind of fun. It's being aware of everything that's going on, being mindful of what other people are doing and what I'm doing, so I can see what needs to be done. It's not personal; if I see there's something that needs to be taken care of, I step in and do it. If someone else steps in and does it, I move on and do something else. It's real different from having everything planned and figured out and going in there and doing what you're told to do — it's like stepping into life knowing that whatever comes up, there's something in myself who's going to do what needs to be done. So now clean-up has this meaning for me — it's a way to learn about right action.

Diane: My first impression of clean-up was exactly the opposite. I was absolutely awed by the precision. I didn't see chaos.

Greg: Much more accurate . . .

Cheri: Objectively speaking, of course. [Laughter]

Cameron: Obviously we each have our own experiences of this. When I first came, I felt awkward about not knowing what to do. So I would find one little thing to do, and do that because it felt comfortable, and while I was doing that, I would see how other things were done. Then next time, I would do what I saw somebody else do. I made it a point to do every task so I could feel comfortable with the whole thing.

Diane: That's kind of how I did it, too, watching to see how it was done. The trouble is, sometimes one person does it one way, and another person does something else.

Terry: I see how I watch others and abandon myself by not having the faith that I will know what to do. To know that I'm going to make mistakes, and in that moment when I'm on the edge, to allow myself to follow my heart anyway, for me that's a hard place. And that's the training.

Cheri: Then add that you might get yelled at if you do it wrong. That's a huge part of it, isn't it?

Terry: It is. That's why there's so much pressure to do it right.

Sara: The guide yells at you?

Cheri: Yes.

Cameron [to Cheri]: "Getting yelled at" is is what people say, and it seems to make sense to everybody, but I've never heard you yell.

Terry: It seems like yelling to the part of me that feels about four years old, that frightened, hurt part of myself, that small child being chastised. I don't enjoy being yelled at. Everything in me wants to withdraw. That's my major defense. The first time it happened, my job was painting Cameron's hermitage, so I was able to go hide in the bushes and paint the house, and that's what I did for two hours. I felt like withdrawing from the world, so that I could be safe. Then another subpersonality came up, the angry defender, which gave me all the reasons why the guide was wrong. So I could just hate her. By this time, I'd forgotten what I'd been yelled at about. I'd gotten totally involved in hurt, withdrawal, anger, hating.

Each time, I go through the same process. The hating seems to get to an extreme point, where I hate everything around me, everything and everybody, and then when I can no longer drum up any more hate, a shift happens, and there's compassion for the part of myself who's doing all that hating. Then it just falls away. Usually that happens in an evening meditation after I've been hating all day.

That first time took about three days of hating. Now I go through that same process in much less time. And I watch it, so it's pretty familiar now.

Jennifer: To me, that says a lot about the value of training in silence. If I wasn't being silent, I couldn't see all that going on. I would see something I thought of as external, someone doing something, and I would attempt to fix it and make it right so I could go on to the next thing to fix.

Even with little things. My most recent one is, because it's winter the dishtowels don't dry out, so what we've got in the kitchen to dry dishes with is lots of wet dishtowels hanging around. I'm supposed to oversee the kitchen, and that includes those wet dishtowels hanging there, and I watch my need to do something about it. What is the most clever thing I can come up with? — so somebody will look at it and say, "That's a clever thing she thought of to do with those wet dishtowels." Even with something simple like that, having to deal with it in silence means I can't ask somebody else to take care of it, I can't complain about it, there isn't anything to do.

And it's fascinating — going through that kind of process is valuable.

Sara: How does that work?

Jennifer: Probably the biggest thing for me is the assumption that something's wrong with the dishtowels being wet. I watch how I do that — thinking that something is wrong, therefore I have to fix it, and then it will be fine and I'll be safe and nothing will ever happen again that's wrong — that kind of sequence. If I can watch myself go through that and step away, some kind of answer becomes obvious. With the dishtowels, it could be to hang them in the sun. But I don't get to that point until I've been able to see that whole process I go through. They can sit there for a week being wet while I'm worrying about thinking up something clever, and I'll replace them sometimes and kind of hide the wet ones, but the fresh ones get wet almost immediately, so then I have two sets of wet dishtowels . . .

Cheri: And then the guide walks in and says, "Why are all these wet dishtowels in here?" I'm just pointing out that this is my job — to say the obvious, unpleasant thing.

Jennifer: And no matter how many things I could fix up and take care of before the guide gets here, she'll always find something else. There were what — four things you pointed out to me at lunch today? Which of course is her job. At some point in seeing that pressure I put on myself, I have to let go the idea that I can possibly keep up. I can't do it all right. So maybe I should just start leaving things around . . .

Diane: In advertising we call it "the hairy arm." On a model's arm, you leave it hairy so the client will have something to pick at and will leave the rest of it alone.

Phyllis: So you plan it in advance to divert attention from —
that could be useful . . .

Cheri [feigning fierceness]: We'll talk later about this.
[Laughter]

✺

The Hardest Things

. . . If we turn inward and prove our True-nature—
that True-self is no-self,
our own Self is no-self—
we go beyond ego and past clever words.
Then the gate to the oneness of cause-and-effect
is thrown open.

Zen Master Hakuin

Sara: How was coming here different from what you expected?

Cameron: The hardest thing for me has been that I did not expect to relinquish control over my life. Here I don't get to make decisions about what I do, and my ego really screams at that. Sometimes I think that this is all wrong, I even think there's something cultish about it. I think I should make my own decisions. Being a person who had always looked toward others, I was trying to develop more autonomy in myself, and now all of a sudden — I don't get to do anything my way. So there's a lot of struggle going on.

Terry: When I'm told to do something I don't want to do, not pursuing my resistance to that but instead going off alone and looking at it — that's a very big part of being here. Because the whole idea is to give up that control, or that illusion of control, which has been so strongly held as a defense.

Sara: Both you and Cameron have talked about having a feeling of "leave me alone." Can you say something about what it's like when you get free of that? What happens then?

Cameron: I don't know if I can articulate it. Usually I feel kind of like I've gone over the top of a mountain, and then I'm seeing clearly. At some point, I get it that it was ego that was locked in a struggle. At the top I realize there's something other than ego, bigger than ego, and that I need to go through these struggles to see how the ego is containing me, in a much more limited way than I really exist. When I get there, I can see how ego works — until the next time, and then it grabs me again.

Terry: For me, it's that struggle in which my major defense is withdrawal. I want my independence, but independence is also isolation. On the one hand, I think what I'm doing is protecting myself, in order to be free, but it's the furthest thing from freedom. There's no feeling of intimacy with myself. I'm isolated, I'm saying I'm independent, but I'm out there all alone and I'm suffering, I'm not connected with myself or with anything. Then when I'm pushed up against it to the point where I can suffer no longer, ego lets go, the heart opens, and it opens to a combination of intimacy and freedom. I realize I'm the only one that's keeping me from it.

Then I start it all up again, I dig in my heels, and it escalates until I reach that same point. But it doesn't take as long as it used to to get to that point of letting go.

Diane: Part of the whole process is to include everything in our spiritual practice. We think resistance and unwillingness are outside spiritual practice; we see them as separate. But as soon as I remember to include all of that, there's a shift.

Let's say spiritual practice lives in my heart, which ostensibly is a very vulnerable place. I want to keep things away that seem dangerous to my heart. But the moment I include that thing I've labeled as "dangerous" and bring it in close to my heart, that label comes off. I liken those labels coming off to taking your shoes off before you enter the meditation hall. Just before something I've identified as separate from me becomes part of my heart, when that label falls off, one part of me says, "Well, it's become acceptance." But that's a label too, and labelling keeps it separate. The only thing I can think of to call this experience is "includedness," which is as close as I can get to not labelling any of it.

Jennifer: That's the main thing for me, that includedness. Ego is afraid it is going to die, afraid it won't have a part anymore, and the way it wants to have a part is to be in control, to be in charge, to make decisions. There's no convincing it that it won't die; there's the constant looking, struggling, letting go, and allowing ego to be a part of that letting go. So maybe a decision will be made or maybe it won't be made, and maybe ego won't get to make it, but ego still gets to be included in that somehow. In that freedom, it feels included; it doesn't feel like it's been killed off or gotten rid of.

Something that's happened for me is that quotations from my background as being raised a Christian come floating through. I used to hate that, because I didn't think they meant anything and I didn't like what they were saying. The quotation that comes to mind most often being in this environment is about giving up your life in order to gain it. I hated that one because there was no way ego was about to do that. Now it's fun to come full cycle and watch those same things come up, but having a different experience of giving up my life in order to gain it. My mother would love this — I've even taken the Bible out on occasion and started re-translating it, taking those words and bringing them back in here to my heart.

Diane: Thinking about ego death, some years ago the guide said to me, "You know, you and I have been working together a long time. I was just wondering at what point you are going to make Buddhism the center of your life instead of your hobby." I walked away from that guidance appointment, and I cried. For the next two days I cried. Then I went back for another guidance appointment, and she said, "Well, what do you suppose this is?" I said, "It feels like death."

My ego was clearly not going to take any of that lying

down. For the next few years, before I made the decision to come here, I went through four jobs, I went through two relationships, I went through one broken bone, I went through major surgery — ego was doing everything possible to keep things stirred up so it wouldn't have to die. When I finally quit the fourth job last September, intuition just said: Now. It was fascinating how frantically ego struggled with what it saw as death for three years, until I was suffering so badly that there was no place else to go but here. There was no freedom in that. It was awful. It was probably one of the worst straitjackets I've ever been in.

Terry: I'm thinking while you're talking about ego death that what I'm doing this month is a lot of grieving. There's a lot of loss and sadness going on, and some of it I can't articulate — it just seems that the body is crying. It doesn't seem to be an intellectual thing, it's a grieving that's going on in my heart.

Every day I'm here, more of me is dying, I'm facing more death. Being willing to let go of the conditioning as much as I'm able in that moment, there's release and freedom, and there's also a grieving.

This practice puts me in touch with the compassionate way of being with loss. That's what growth is beginning to feel like: grieving for loss day after day, and the compassion building as the loss grows, as there's more and more letting go of identity. I'm feeling like, this is the hard part for me, this is the work, to feel the hurt, the pain, the vulnerability, but staying open and not closing.

I watch myself go through the day, and the tendency is to want to close around the pain, to defend myself. It comes out in ways like mentally criticizing what someone else is doing, in order to distance myself, to separate myself. When that happens, I remind myself to try to stay open. I find the fear is that as long as I stay open, there will be more pain and I won't survive. But what I am open to also is the compassion. No matter how much pain comes in, the compassion is there too, as long as I stay open.

Greg: My experience of coming here was not coming to a place where I was being rigidly controlled. That was what I wanted — to have a set of clear rules I could follow perfectly. That's why I love [the writings of Zen Master] Dogen so much, because everything's there: how you cook, how you do this, how you do that. I was hoping we would have that here. So I haven't felt forced to do things I don't want to do, because if you would tell me what you wanted me to do, I would love it. I really wanted to know, in such and such situation, that the right thing to do, or the compassionate thing to do, or whatever word you want — meaning the safe way to do it — is such and such. But that's never been given to me here. For me, it's been the opposite — it's not possible to know what's good, not possible to know what's the right way to act.

I used to complain about there not being enough rules, and the guide would tell me that if this place wasn't strict enough for me, she'd send me to her teacher. So my experience was not walking into a controlled environment, but walking into craziness, people doing things that seemed clearly wrong to me. And when I'd complain about it, I'd get into trouble.

So I have had to explore that. I found that in wanting rules, I was looking for something that would take away the pressure, because inside of me is a set of rules so strict that there isn't any way to win, there isn't any way to be right. Before I came here, I just operated according to those rules, without knowing what they were. And it always felt like — I lost. Then I came here and tried to find another set of rules that would make it possible to win. And it became clear that there was no such thing.

So now I look at the rules I make up for myself. What are the ways I set things up so I'll always lose? Would it be possible to let myself simply respond to what is? The direction all this led to for me is responding to what is happening in the moment.

Jennifer: I have an experience similar to Greg's. I was sure that I was in the right place because when I came here, there was a set of rules. I think Greg must have written them up . . .

Greg: I did!

Jennifer: . . . and I knew I had found home, because there was somebody here who saw things the same way I did. So I set out to follow those rules and immediately found out the same things he did. . .

Cameron: Could I take a look at those rules? [Laughter]

Jennifer: Actually, they're all neatly printed out from a computer now. I remember thinking if I could just follow those perfectly then I would be good and everything would be fine, people would like me, and I would be safe. When I wasn't able to follow them perfectly and I got into trouble, then I started telling on other people who didn't follow them. And I still got into trouble.

Then I started to wonder what the constant was in the picture. I began to look inside to see where my own rules came from, then I had to look at fear. Behind the "what if —?" questions was fear. What if I did it differently? What if I let go the part of me that thinks things have to be a certain way? Right on the heels of that would be, "Well, if you let go of fear, then you'd be doing it perfect and right and good." That idea was always there, and still is.

The most wonderful thing now is learning to just live with that fear. The fear has to be part of it all, something I wouldn't try to push away—but not identifying with it either, knowing that that's not who I am, it's just part of conditioning.

Following the rules doesn't take care of it, and not following the rules doesn't take care of it — although I'm working more on not following the rules just to see how that feels.

Phyllis: I like following rules and I like doing things right, but I have this other thing of wanting to go beyond the rules, to the spirit of it all. Yet somehow for the first year particularly, I came up against a wall at every turn. I couldn't follow the rules, really, because I couldn't get inside Greg and Jennifer's heads, which is where the rules were. [Laughter] I was following my own interpretation, which was always "wrong."

Greg: But not even we could follow the rules.

Phyllis: I know. At that point, Jennifer was in charge. Jennifer was the one who told us what to do, and that was very difficult because — I didn't like Jennifer telling me what to do. And then knowing that I wasn't doing it "right" [pointing to Greg] — that's the other side of it. So it was a constant state of confusion for me . . .

Greg: You never asked me, Phyl, or I would have told you how to do things.

Phyllis: Yes, you would. Especially after the fact. But then my ego would be up on its high horse. So it was a constant state of not being able to do anything right, not wanting to do anything — I mean I did it, but not wanting to — everything being hard, having my own internal stuff of, "I can't," and "It's too hard," and "It's too hot," and "It's too cold," and that went on for the whole first year. It was a very difficult year.

Before I came here I was leading a religious life and it was pretty intense in the beginning, but as time went on, I would describe it as kind of lukewarm. There's a gospel passage that always made me nervous, something about, "If you're lukewarm, I'll vomit you out." I wouldn't look at that in myself at the time, but I was that way.

So I got to this place, and there was nothing really wrong, there wasn't huge suffering, but nothing really right either. That first year, all my crabby subpersonalities were out, and I was supposed to be accepting that, which was difficult, because, I thought, "I'm not this way; I've never been this way before."

One of the biggest things for me was getting the job of moving the lumber yard. It was supposed to be two of us, but only one of us was really doing it, and it was me. Moving the whole lumber yard day after day after day. Like Sisyphus. It was summer, and it was hot, day after day after day . . .

Greg: What you didn't know was that every evening we carried it all back again.

Phyllis: I believe it. I was the cook that year also, and the pressure was on. It seemed like things were impossible, until finally — this is why I hope people stay long enough — finally I stopped resisting it. And you know, now cold is only cold, hot is only hot, work is only work, hard is only hard, misery is only misery. It's completely different from how I was doing all that resistance. And fun — now everything's always fun. That's how I would describe being here. It doesn't mean it's not hard and miserable and all that sometimes, but it's still fun.

I thank God that I lasted through that point. Because I could see that when people leave before that — it was just so awful. And yet there was nothing awful happening. I was making it awful. For me there's the whole other side of what happens after you quit resisting — ego is still there, it hasn't given up, but it's lost its hold. I can look at it and know its tricks.

I have a fond memory of moving the lumber yard because that gave me a big push toward letting go. And everything around — I'd look at the ants and say, "Gee, I'm just like those ants" — you know, when it came to moving the lumber yard. That was a huge step for me in giving up that resistance.

Greg: I continue to have the kind of experiences Phyl talked about with the lumber yard, where the resistance is just as strong. But the difference is that having that resistance doesn't really matter.

The example that comes to mind is that we have had a number of storms blow down our kitchen tent. And it never happens at eleven in the morning; it's always something like one a.m. There's a way in which times like that are incredibly fun, because it's raining and cold and miserable but we're all working together, pulling up the kitchen tent. Parts of me are resisting like crazy, but they're only part of the whole experience. I've gotten to a point where it isn't worth it to give in to the resistance, to stop doing what needs to be done just because there's someone inside of me who doesn't want to do it.

So now, even though I feel quite miserable, there's a whole different quality to that misery, and there is a sense of enjoyment — not enjoying the fact that part of me is miserable but enjoying the room for that one to go ahead and be miserable.

One of my favorite things in saying the Daily Recollection is "O happy blessed opportunity." Every difficult situation is an opportunity to end suffering, if only I stick around long enough to examine that big bunch of resistance — because the resistance is the suffering. My experience is that when I look at resistance, it ceases to be "mine"; it just is, and it becomes something to work with rather than suffer over.

❂

Teaching What You Need to Learn

Thus, words are bits and pieces of leaping out; teacher and disciple practice mutually. What is heard is bits and pieces leaping out; teacher and disciple practice mutually.

"Teacher and disciple practice mutually" is twining vines of buddha ancestors.

Zen Master Dogen

Sara: I know Phyllis and Greg and Jennifer have been leading groups down at the Zen Center, and I'm curious to know what that's like, becoming a teacher yourself.

Greg: Well, I didn't . . . [Laughs].

Cheri: You didn't realize that was your function? You thought you were just keeping the cushion warm until the teacher got there?

Sara: Oh—you haven't thought of yourself as a teacher? [Greg shakes his head.] Because the people at the Zen Center think of you as teachers.

Phyllis: For me, being in that position has made me do my practice much harder than I would have otherwise. You have to be continually watching, because you won't have anything to give unless you're paying attention. It feels like a big responsibility, and also it's an invaluable learning experience.

I taught children for many years, so teaching has been part of my life. But I also have this voice that tells me "I can't"— a belief that I can't do various things. Especially I felt I couldn't do things involving adults. One of the first things the guide asked me to do was be the work director at our retreat in Carmel. I immediately thought, "I can't." But by then I wasn't afraid of grown-ups anymore. I mean, I've been a grown-up for all these years now, and also I had caught on to the "I can't" voice. So she asked me, and I knew I could do it, because of where I was in my spiritual training. Yet those voices kept coming up to say I couldn't.

At the Zen Center, leading discussion groups or giving individual guidance, the funny thing is, I sit there in that room doing it and hearing myself say, "I can't." Obviously I am doing it. And even enjoying it, because now I sit there almost laughing at myself. I know I'm just one of this group, I'm not the teacher; it's just that this is the particular cushion I have been asked to sit on at this time. Most of the people there could trade places with me. I think having that outlook on it has been a help, because then I don't have a lot of expectations of myself to produce something. What comes out comes out, and what doesn't doesn't.

Greg: Jennifer and I lead a meditation workshop, and preparing for that really helped my practice — just trying to figure out what is this we do, anyway? Is posture important? And breathing? That sort of thing. Terry and I do another one that's very helpful on identity mapping. It keeps me aware of things that I might otherwise forget, because I have to talk about them. I keep watching my posture and watching my process a little bit harder because if I'm going to be talking about something I need to know my own experience of it.

Another aspect of it is something our teacher quotes her teacher as saying: you'll do for the love of others what you would not do for yourself. A lot of times in leading a group I'm trying to do a "good job," trying to get something across, and that usually doesn't help. But every once in a while I'll respond to somebody or a situation in a way that is clear, and then I realize I've just learned something. It's not that I knew something that I had to teach somebody, but I learned something that I need to practice. So being in that teacher role can be difficult for the part of me who doesn't want to practice.

That part of me would just as soon not hear some of the things that I have to say.

Terry: I'm finding that when I lead workshops I'm required to pay much closer attention. I'm required to pay attention for the whole duration and to expand my awareness to everyone's reaction in the room, including mine, in that moment. Then I'm required to let that go completely, and move on to the next moment. Every time I facilitate a workshop, I go away with the sense that I have paid closer attention for that length of time than ever before in my life.

And I'm learning that I can do that not only for the other person, but for myself. It has shown me how I don't listen to my own heart, how I abandon myself simply by not listening. In teaching there is the requirement to be there for somebody else, which I'll often deny to myself. But when I'm paying attention with my heart, it's just this being [points to herself] doing this practice. Coming from the heart. I'm talking to you, but I'm really talking to me: in that moment, there is no separation. It's so obvious that you teach what you need to learn.

Jennifer: Facilitating group discussions has also been one of the best opportunities for me to learn. I also taught young children for a number of years, and my identity was tied up with that: teaching was something I could do and do well, something I knew about. So I brought with me that notion that I knew something, but I realized quickly how it gets in the way. So I've struggled with having to put that aside — not kick it out, but compassionately set it aside so that I could really facilitate a group discussion. Putting it aside leaves me knowing that I don't know anything, that my mind doesn't have information or answers for somebody else. The best I can do is be with someone and pay attention. Doing that over and over again has been really valuable to me.

Cheri: So your ego becomes one of the persons in the group who needs the same kind of attention as any of the others.

Jennifer: Yes. In setting it aside, it becomes just like someone else—not something I want to get rid of or that I identify with, and not a perspective I try and teach from, but someone else who needs love and compassion.

Terry: At certain points when I'm asking other people in the group to comment, I'm so enthralled with what's going on that I forget that I'm the facilitator. When the other person finishes, there's this moment before I realize, "Oh, it's back to me." Because there's a letting go of this identity, and all of a sudden I'm just one of those people.

Jennifer: I had a good experience of the opposite of that. At my first guidance appointment after I moved here to the monastery, the guide asked me to be the guest master. I knew that I couldn't say no. And when I said yes, it was with real enthusiasm. That came from thinking I needed to have an important job, and here she was providing it for me. I was really excited about it, but when we finished talking and she left, I realized she didn't tell me what the guest master does. She didn't give me a job description.

Right then I became afraid of doing it wrong. For about two years I had that job, and not once during that time could I get the guide to tell me what it meant. I still haven't. The learning was in watching myself having that job and needing to be important: I got to see how I do that kind of thing.

Another wonderful thing was that in the same way the job was offered, it was taken away; in that same flow of transition — no big deal that I got it, no big deal that I'm not doing it anymore. And I had the same opportunity when she took it away as when it was offered — to watch how attached I was: there goes my identity, my importance. The same thing replayed again, and watching that helps with being humble and with letting go any idea of feeling important about anything. At the same time, the part of me that has that identity needs to be taken care of, in the same way that I would compassionately care for someone else.

Terry: When Greg and I do a workshop, it's different every time, and we never know what we're going to get or how we're going to process it. But I have complete confidence that one of us will come up with something. Because people seem to need to hear things said in different ways, it just works out. If I'm responding to someone and it doesn't seem to be going anywhere, then Greg may say the same thing in a different way, coming from a different perspective, and then it will click for that person.

Diane: That has been useful to me in being here and listening to Greg and Phyl and Jennifer in group discussions on Sunday. Hearing it with different words makes things resonate in a new way. I think of the story about the monk who achieved enlightenment because somebody behind him dropped a pebble, so he founded an entire monastery where people walk up behind each other and drop pebbles. It's so self-focused to think that whatever it is that resonated for you will resonate for somebody else; it's not necessarily true. For me it's helpful to be in an environment where I can hear other people talk about doing this process. I have this wonderful experience of seeing the teacher and seeing students of the teacher, and those students being teachers for me.

❂

Living the Precepts

Wrong is not always wrong, nor right always right. If you cling to fixed ideas, a tenth of an inch's difference will set you ten thousand miles away.

Yoka-daishi, Song of Realization

Phyllis: Taking the precepts is like a formal, public acceptance and commitment to keep those precepts. Of course any commitment we make, we have to make every day, every moment. Doing it publicly brings out different aspects of those vows. It certainly has for the people who have come here to the precepts ceremony and the precepts workshops. We've had very interesting discussions around the precepts.

Jennifer: My feeling about the ceremony was that it was like a conscious baptism. It was the public acceptance of something I had wanted for a long time. It didn't mean that I would keep the precepts perfectly. It meant that I would use them as guidelines to live my life and do that as compassionately as I could, and that I was willing to say that in front of other people. It felt as close to something sacred as I could ever get.

Terry: When I took the precepts, the night before the ceremony we wrote out all the things we forgave ourselves for — and not just ourselves, but everybody, everything we could think of, and during the ceremony, we let go of all those things. That had a great impact on me. I wasn't expecting forgiveness. I felt elated.

I see taking the precepts as a promise, a promise to myself. The precepts are guidelines for ending suffering, and I have made the promise to myself to end suffering for this person. I've made the promise not to abandon myself. When I break that promise, the one person whose life it affects is this one. But this practice helps me keep that promise. And that's the joy of doing this publicly, joining with so many people who also see it as a path to end suffering.

Jennifer: One thing that seems to come up for people before the ceremony is the notion of having these things we say we'll do, and then what if we can't keep them the way we think we should? It's that agony about wanting to do it right. One person who was getting ready to take the precepts said she could accept all of them but one, the one about not taking intoxicating drinks or narcotics. She said, "I'm clear about it, I'm going to have a beer sometimes." So we looked at that. Here's this precept that says one thing, and here I am knowing what I am willing to do, and these things look very different.

I remember Greg talking with her about backing it up to find at what point the abandonment of herself occurs, and finding the willingness to have compassion for the part of herself who was struggling with these two things that she couldn't reconcile. To have compassion for that part of us *is* keeping that precept. She also saw that maybe at some point she would choose not to have the beer — but that only followed from having compassion for the one who still wanted to and was struggling because it looked like she had to stop.

It isn't about keeping the letter of the law. That was an eye-opener for me, having a strong subpersonality who loves the letter of the law. The suffering, for me, comes from the one who wants so desperately to get it right and who is afraid that if I don't, something awful is going to happen. I was thinking about what Terry said about abandoning ourselves. I promise that I won't abandon myself, and yet when I do abandon myself, I promise that I'll keep looking and have compassion for the one that just abandoned myself. Or just had a beer, or whatever it is. Having that compassion is actually keeping the precepts.

Sara: Could you explain the process of "backing it up" to that point?

Jennifer: One of the precepts is not to lead a harmful life. First, I would have ideas about what harmfulness means — killing a mosquito, for a real example. So part of me says, "That's a harmful act." Then if I step back, I see that I've judged myself for committing this harmful act, which goes against this precept. But the *judgment itself* is a harmful act, and that's the harm I need to stop, right then, with compassion. In that same space, there's compassion for judging myself, there's a dead mosquito, and there's the precept — all of that. So backing it up takes us to what underlies what happens, to something deeper than what we think is the issue.

Sara: I see it in that example, but how do you extend that to intoxication?

Phyllis: It's the same. If you held that you had to keep the precepts verbatim, and you weren't going to drink a beer and that was that, and then you drank a beer and you got down on yourself about it, you'd be breaking the precept of not causing harm.

Greg: The point, as I remember it in that case, was asking the person if they are open to the possibility that someday they would pay attention to their experience and maybe decide that they didn't want to drink anymore. For me, to accept the precepts means being willing to pay careful attention to my experience and to be open to the possibility that things can be different. And that person had an aspiration to do this path, but was afraid that she couldn't do it because she couldn't keep that precept to the letter. But she did find a willingness to consider the possibility that some day . . .

Cameron: As I recall it, we also discussed the various meanings of the precept, and that they weren't necessarily literal. We talked about the "wine of delusion" and some of the other meanings besides simply drinking alcohol. We talked about it in a larger perspective.

Phyllis: But no matter how much we talked about it, people would bring it back to drinking a beer and the letter of the law.

Jennifer: And that's where the harmfulness comes in. If I won't have compassion for the one who wants to drink a beer, or who is drinking a beer right now, then I won't be open to the possibility of change. I would just make up another rule for myself. And I might stop drinking beer, but I'd hate it and I'd hate the rule and hate myself. But out of having compassion for the one who wants to do it, then there's that possibility for it to be different. And if what I want to do is end suffering, the stopping would probably just happen, but not because I thought I should stop.

Phyllis: By keeping the precepts as rules and punishing ourselves for breaking them, we're setting ourselves up for not keeping them, for being able to say, "This whole thing is awful, I don't want anything to do with it." I suspect that's what happens with the Ten Commandments as well, which I think are the same kind of guidelines as the precepts. We can look at them like the person looked at drinking beer, and say, I'll either keep that precept or I won't. So if I say that I can't keep it, that means I'm off the hook, I don't have to keep it. If I say I'll keep it and then don't, and I beat myself up about it, that's surely a way of continuing to suffer and eventually not keeping the precept at all.

It's *how* I approach "keeping the precepts" that makes all the difference. *Planning* how I'm going to keep the precepts takes me out of the present moment; it completely closes the door to what could happen in reality, which can be anything. When I finally got it that you don't plan how to keep the precepts, or anything else for that matter, life became much simpler. I can just pay attention in the moment, with an open heart, with the willingness to use the precepts as guidelines for how not to suffer. To have the willingness to not cause harm or not take an intoxicating drink or whatever, and to watch what comes up in the moment, to pay attention, has a whole different effect. I can be in the moment and see what is going on, rather than being caught up in some sphere other than reality — some made-up place in my mind.

Terry: If we take the precepts as rules, two people can do what seems like the same action and it may appear that both of them are breaking a precept — but for one of those people that may be true, and not for the other one. It depends on the attitude of mind, and what's happening in the moment. From that perspective the precepts are very individual. Because how we act in a given situation is based on each of our lifetimes, our own experiences, and what we bring to this present life. So it may look very different, what I do and what Phyl does, and yet we may both be following the precepts.

Making rules is different — it's the mind's effort, so that we can always just do things the same way. But that takes us away from the present moment. The best that I can do is be fully present, and whatever arises, let it be there, not worrying about whether I'm breaking a precept. If I'm there in the moment, then that's all there is, and nothing is going to be broken.

Sara: Could you give an example of something that would look like breaking a precept from the outside and yet . . .

Phyllis: Taking narcotics, a dying person taking morphine, for instance. If somebody is going by the letter of the law, that's breaking a precept. Or someone who is Buddhist having to give a drug in a situation like that. But in that moment, that might well be the compassionate thing to do. So you pay attention and look, because there might have been something you've missed. Rationalization might have set in, you know; it may not have been compassion at all. It's important to pay close attention, before, during, and after.

Greg: If I ever start telling myself how I didn't really break that precept, or try to justify it by saying, "Well, I was being in the moment," that's a sure sign I did break it. Or if I'm looking at something someone else did, and I'm going on and on in my mind about how that person broke that precept — well, who's doing that? I'm doing it.

For me, the precepts are an important part of the package — they're not the whole package. Everything in the Daily Recollection goes together, and you can't do the precepts without doing all the rest of it. For example, there's a section after the precepts where we talk about practicing lovingkindness, pure attention, ever-expanding faith, constant devotion, and inquiry through correct meditation. Unless you're doing those five things, you cannot possibly follow the precepts. If to your view you never harm anything, never tell lies, never do this, that and the other thing, and you don't practice lovingkindness, then you're missing something. I don't see how people who don't practice meditation all the time could ever worry about precepts. That's why, I guess, the precepts aren't talked about very much until someone is a long way into this, because how do you tell the difference between a precept and a rule unless you can pay attention to your experience?

It's like this: I know when I've broken a precept by an experience of suffering inside me. That's how I know that it happened. And until I learned to pay attention to that, even to notice suffering at all, things were just rules. Even though we call it the ceremony of accepting the precepts, it's actually the ceremony of expressing your willingness to pay attention to your experience, or to do your best to live compassionately in the present moment. The way I've looked at the actual Ten Grave Prohibitive Precepts is, okay, you've decided you want to stop suffering. So why don't you see what happens if you try not doing these things? And then you could also see what happens if you do these things. Pay careful attention and see what happens when you lie, see what happens when you don't lie. Which do you like best? Although I may not suffer as a result of telling that lie, that doesn't mean there aren't any consequences. You don't get to a point where you can break precepts and you're free from consequences because you're "enlightened."

Another part for me is in St. Paul, where he says, in effect, "I can't believe all these bad things I do, and I can't seem to help it." That's my experience a lot. Even when my actions seem to be in keeping with the precepts, my experience is that I constantly fail to keep them. But that's not a problem, because it means I'm constantly seeing at deeper and deeper levels how I break the precepts. The whole idea of being here is to notice how I suffer. So, although I may not go around saying bad things about people, in my head I'm doing it all the time, breaking that precept. I can't say to myself, "I didn't say that out loud, so everything's cool." Because when I look at what this does inside me, I see suffering. When I am grumbling about somebody, I am in fact suffering. The closer I get to my experience, the more I see that happen.

There's that thing in Buddhism, the Four Great Vows that I can't remember, so I invented in place of them what I call the One Giant Paraphrase, which is, "This path is impossible; I vow to do it." These precepts are impossible, I vow to keep them. If I can't see how I'm breaking the precepts, then I'm probably not paying attention.

Phyllis: It's what we call "going farther and faring worse." The more I look, the more I meditate, the clearer things become — the more I realize that breaking the precepts goes on constantly, all the time. This is good; it's the beginning of humility. I just see more, so that subtleties I wouldn't have noticed a while ago become causes for suffering. Many times, breaking the precepts helps to catch my attention. What I have done brings me up short, catches me in the face, so I have to look at it. Thus I begin to see it more clearly. Guidance is important in helping you not get stuck at the point of feeling "bad" or "wrong" for breaking a precept rather than learning from that particular opportunity.

Greg: We get this paper, the *National Catholic Reporter*. A couple of weeks ago there was an issue that showed pictures of the group of Jesuits and their housekeepers who were killed in El Salvador. The first thing that happened in me was anger at the murderers. But then I knew exactly how it was possible for those murderers to do what they did — because I did it myself, I did it right then in my mind as I looked at that picture. I murdered the murderers.

It becomes very hard to judge people — not that I don't try — when I see how I do the same things they do. It's possible to know how any kind of atrocity can happen, because I may do it in a little way and somebody else did it in a big way, but I still do it, I know how it happens. That's why it seems like it would be awful for someone to be able to keep the precepts perfectly. It might be okay if they did it perfectly after maybe sixty or eighty years or many lifetimes of long, hard work, but to be able to say, "Oh, okay, I'll just do them perfectly" — that person would be worthless. They couldn't understand anyone else's experience.

Terry: Because you have to go to that place of compassion and really be that experience, whatever it is — Greg going within himself and being the experience of the people who murdered —before there can be that degree of compassion. The compassion is always there, because that's True Nature, but in order to get to those deeper levels, it's necessary to go to all the experiences of suffering that we can possibly have in order to know the depth of compassion.

Sara: So trying to keep the precepts is not so important as using them as a way of seeing what goes on with you and how suffering happens. Not that you don't try, but that the point of the trying and failing . . .

Greg: It's not a scorecard.

Phyllis: Using them in the way you describe *is* what I call keeping them. It is part and parcel of keeping them. The outcome will be a compassionate keeping of the precepts.

Terry: You can look at it in terms of goodness. If I keep the precepts and then want my reward, it misses the point. And in fact, there's nothing there. But if I'm doing goodness for its own sake, that is the reward. It's in the doing itself.

Phyllis: It brings to mind for me the parable of the talents, where the one servant got ten talents, one got five, and one got one, and the one with ten invested and made another ten, and the one with five invested and made another five, and the one with one was so afraid of losing it he buried it. And when the Master returned, he praised the first and second ones for using the talents and making more. And to the last one he said, "What did you do with yours?" And the servant said, "You're such a hard taskmaster and I was so afraid of you that I buried it so I would have it to give back to you, and here it is." And the Master said, "You worthless servant, give your one to the ones who made more." That parable always made me feel uneasy.

Now, when I look at it in relation to keeping the precepts, I realize that "keeping them," in the narrow sense, is not unlike the "burying of the talents" in the parable. By keeping them, burying them, nothing grows from them, they become sterile — instead of using them, not being afraid to step out there in the world and have them as growing, living things. Which involves risk and making mistakes.

❂

Sangha

To study the Way is to study the self.
To study the self is to forget the self.
To forget the self is to be enlightened by all things.
To be enlightened by all things is to remove the barriers
  between one's self and others.

We take refuge in the Buddha because he is our great teacher.
We take refuge in the Law [Dharma] because it is good
medicine. We take refuge in the Buddhist community
[Sangha] because it is composed of excellent friends.

Zen Master Dogen

Greg: The main thing for me that is different from living in the world is that our sangha is made of people who have principally agreed to pay attention to what we do, how we do things. We don't agree to a certain set of rules, only guidelines, but we agree to take responsibility for our experience, to the best of our ability.

There have been times when each of the three of us has been through a kind of breakdown — I imagine like they put you in mental hospitals for. I go into severe depressions, and Phyl does what she does, and Jennifer does what she does. The agreement we have here is to let people go through what they need to go through. Because sending people to mental hospitals stops the process. What we learn here is, you go down and then you come up again. The mental hospital just gets in the way: you go down, they put you on drugs, and that stops everything. I'm so grateful that this is an environment where people will let you go ahead and be a total jerk, because you have to do that stuff in order to know how you do it.

We try our best not to act out, but to be watching our internal experience. But the acting out happens. Often when one person is completely messed up, another person is clear, so when you try to bite their head off, they just let it happen without taking it personally. That aspect of being involved with each other while not taking each other personally is so valuable. It's not until I watch myself treat someone badly, either in my mind or in my actions, that I discover what effect it has — not on the other person, but on me. If I treat someone badly and they do something back, then I get to be mad about it and never see what's at the root of what I did. Whereas my experience indicates that if I truly understand and accept the parts of me that treat people badly, I do not want to treat people badly. And I am open to compassion for those who treat me badly.

Phyllis: I've lived in community since I was about eighteen, and it's that not taking things personally and the understanding of projection that makes my experience of sangha different here. And also the silence. In my previous community, after we stopped keeping the silence, things became very personal and personality-oriented. Here, doing this kind of practice where people know how not to take things personally and know about projection and know that whatever goes on is a mirror of themselves, that's what makes this community work.

Jennifer: Something I used to be confused about was that a part of me wanted this training to be a very personal thing. Guidance with the teacher felt very personal, and learning to meditate and going to groups was all very personal; there were connections to be made with people and that was what I had been looking for.

Then at some point, I realized that the personal quality I had been looking for wasn't really what I had thought. I was looking for intimacy, and where I hadn't found it was in myself; I had not developed that kind of relationship with myself. And because I hadn't found it within, I also didn't have it in my life, and I would go around looking for it with this

154

person or this family or this community or whatever, and not find it. Once I could see that it's the ego that wants to be personal about everything, then I could begin to let that go, and right behind it is true intimacy, in a much fuller, deeper sense of the word "personal" than I knew was possible.

So definitions also began changing for me, in terms of personal and intimacy and relationships and probably just about everything I could think of. Because of the silence and the support of doing the practice and paying attention, that kind of shift can happen. I have found the things I was looking for, but in a whole different way than I thought it would be.

Terry: I remember talking to Phyl before I came here and saying that one of my hesitancies about coming was that before I went away to a monastery, I wanted just once to have a healthy relationship. And she said to me, "You're going to have a relationship with the one person who matters — yourself."

Now, I am finding here within myself what I had been searching for out there in somebody else. What makes it possible for me is the support of other people doing the practice, and the silence. In any other environment I would be able to challenge other people verbally. Here I can't do that, so I'm forced to look at myself. I am in that intimate relationship right here, as I see everything going on within me.

Once a week I also have the opportunity of being with the Zen Center part of the sangha. So I get to be with the people I live with here and with the people I trained with two years there. And the combination of those two just reinforces to me how important the sangha is and how hard it is to train without it.

Sara: Over the years you've had people go as well as come, and recently Tom left. How has that affected the sense of sangha? What has it meant to have someone leave?

155

Phyllis: For me there were two different instances, when Peter left and when Tom left. When Peter left, it felt kind of finished, he seemed ready, he had developed quite a bit and could now make it in the world. In some ways there was a sense of loss, and yet in other ways for me it felt like this was what he needed to do and it was fine. For Tom it was a whole different thing. I feel like just from the little I know of Tom, that if he's going to make it, this is where he would be able to make it, if he were going to become a whole, happy, healthy person, it would be here. He might be able to go out there and be fine, but my projection is that he will do whatever he does to make himself unhappy. That would be the best that would happen. That he ran away at that point we've all experienced of complete, intense misery, rather than going through that suffering, leaves me with a real sense of sadness.

Jennifer: It was a very sad thing for me, too. It was like somebody in my family died, and that's because of the intimacy that's here. What I keep projecting is, if I had left here at a certain point in my training that was very difficult for me, it would have been with the thought that there was somewhere else to go, that I could have gotten away from the very things I needed to face. That's what leaving here represented for me then, and that's what I project about Tom. I would have thought that I could get away from myself or that this place wasn't where I needed to be, and I would have had to go somewhere else to run up against myself again to find out that that wasn't true.

It's not that we're here forever and we can't leave. But as Phyl was saying, it's important to stay with a difficult experience all the way through, knowing that there isn't anywhere to go—that where I am, there I am. To have believed the voices saying, "You need to go," to leave thinking I could find something else, imagining that I would be content, and yet knowing that that isn't true — that feels like suffering to me.

Greg: Since I've been here, four people have come and gone. When the first two people left, I felt crushed. I was sure that would be the end of them, and I felt fear that something awful could happen to me—I could make a mistake or do something wrong and then have to go.

Then it shifted for me; there's part of me that feels sad when people go, and part of me understands that it might be necessary for them to try out a lot of things. I've tried so many things—and had a whole lot of them not work, so I don't need to try anything else. But if I hadn't done all the trying and running into walls, I wouldn't have been sure that this is what I want to do. And so my hope is that when people leave that they're just finding out more about what doesn't work for them, and maybe at some point of going through this however many times it takes, they will find out what does.

It's like most people have to figure out every way it's possible to suffer, figure out all the things that cause suffering, and finally reach a point where they know, "Okay, that's enough suffering, and now I'm going to do something differently." It seems as if it's necessary to go through the whole process until you're convinced. So, I wouldn't want people to stay here not being convinced that it was the most appropriate thing for them to be doing at the moment.

I worry about people when they go, a little bit. But I take responsibility for those projections. I have hopes that they will find what they're looking for, and I don't feel it's a tragedy. It used to feel like the most awful thing in the world when someone left, as if they had died.

Terry: Also, people do come here with different commitment levels. I didn't live here when Peter left, but I knew Peter from the sangha and I kind of get the sense that Phyl talks about, that he got what he needed to get and moved on. I can't really know about Tom because I can't talk to him, and I feel a sadness about that.

I think about how Diane will be leaving soon and then Cameron will be leaving after that, and my commitment is for a year, and so I'll be leaving too. When I think about Cameron and Diane leaving sooner than I will, I already feel sad. And thinking that the three of you probably will continue to live here, automatically I feel like — I'm the only short-timer. I don't see myself living in a monastery for all of my life; I don't even know whether after a year I'll want to stay or I'll want to go.

There's no necessity for people to stay here forever, as though at the end of my year here, if I return to the world, I won't be fine. This is a segment of time I set aside for myself to live in this way. It doesn't mean that when you leave here you're not still doing the practice.

Diane: I project, however, that Tom leaving is a very sad thing. I got the job of boxing up all his personal belongings in his hermitage, and I have done that before for friends who have died. That's what it felt like. It was so unfinished. And there's a piece of me that relates so closely to just wanting to run away, to get the hell out of here and protect myself. And, from this projection, that is what happened to Tom.

One of the things I had to store away was a big bulletin board that Tom had, with pictures of himself from the time he was four until recently; there must have been twenty of them. And also on that bulletin board were little post-it notes of things his subpersonalities say. I tried to get a bag over it as quickly as I could so that I wouldn't see all that, because it seemed so private. But as you're trying to get a bag over it you can't keep your eyes closed, so of course I saw some of them. I've tried to block this image out of my mind, one of the phrases there so saddened me. It said, "I've just got to go."

That struck such a chord with me because I know what that feels like. I know that pain. I know what it would be like to leave, and then two days later feel sorry, but knowing I couldn't go back. Or feeling I couldn't — something inside me saying I couldn't. Then you're left with that feeling: I've failed again. So for me, Tom brings up something completely different from Peter, different from limited commitments when you know when you're coming and when you're going. It brings up that piece of me that would like to just run away and not face things anymore.

Terry: It brings that up for me too in how I gave up my job and my home, I said good-bye to my friends and gave all my possessions away to come here —because I'm the person who three days into the retreat says, "I want to go home now." I knew that if I had a place to go to, I might leave. I wondered if I got to that place of extreme misery, if I had a place, would I go home? To see Tom just pick up and go and leave everything here, I thought, "I could still go." That's scary, because Tom's leaving reminds me that I really don't have to stay here. I thought I set it up so I wouldn't have to deal with that, but the truth is, I could go the same way he did, just pick up and leave.

To be able to walk away, knowing you're probably hurting people, knowing you're leaving behind everything that you own — it takes a combination of incredible pain and incredible courage, to be able to do that. When I think about Tom, what comes to my mind is that he probably wouldn't allow himself to come back, because of the way he left. And I think that even though the option of doing it like that is there for me, I could never do it. Leaving would be abandoning myself so much that I don't think I would be able to come back — for that reason, that I would have so completely abandoned myself.

Greg: I used to feel depressed when people left, even after a workshop or retreat, and I'd worry about people who didn't show up for awhile. I would get personally involved in people's lives, in that I believed that the only way a person could be okay was to be here, training, like me. I projected that to go back to the world was a tragedy. But now I really like the impersonalness of it, in the sense that every time somebody comes, or a group comes, it's like they're here to do certain work, which we accomplish, and then we disperse. The constant is people coming here wanting to do this work. Now that's what I enjoy; whoever is here, we're going to practice together, and I always get something out of it. I've lost the desire that everyone come live here, or that everyone all do the same thing. People come, and people leave, and that's just the way it works.

I also lost some of my sense of self-importance when I realized that that would be true for me also — that I am here now, and someday, for whatever reason, I'm not going to be here, and the practice will keep on going. At first that was hard to take, but it's comforting too, to get a larger view of this process, seeing that the characters will change but the training will keep going on.

So I'm glad when people come and we do what we do. It's good. And I'm glad when they leave. The fact that people come and go means that I can't just assume that the work I have to do can be done any time. Things come up, each person provides an opportunity to work with some part of me, with the sensations, emotions, and thoughts that arise, the projections I make, and I might miss an important opportunity if I don't do that when they're here.

Jennifer: Another thing for me is that sangha is everyone and everywhere — not just us here at this monastery and those who practice at other Zen centers. For me, the more that concept expands, the less important I become. That's helped me to see how everyone can be a guide for me and for each other. So in that sense, sangha does not exclude anything. If I chose to leave this place and there's something I could take with me, it would be that notion that wherever I am, I could continue this training, and appreciate everyone and everything I encounter as guidance.

Phyllis: You know yesterday how I was talking about being afraid of grown-ups? It was because I experienced myself as separate from others, I felt a distance from them. And then one day I noticed that everybody — was me. And not only everybody, but everything, like those ants and bugs and so on. And since there is no me, the way that connection is made must be through True Nature. That completely changes how I relate to people. There are no strangers, no "grown-ups" — everyone is a child, so to speak. That is my sense of sangha — it includes people, animals, leaves, anything, and the connection is through True Nature. Obviously that's changed my life quite a bit [laughing].

Terry: I'm going to tell on you, Phyl. I get to talk with Phyl because she's my work director. I walked into the storage shed, and Phyl was talking and there was no one else there. At first I thought she was talking to me, but then I realized she was talking to herself. But she said, "You know, I wasn't talking to me, I was talking to the hammer, the walls, the tree — I'm making that connection with them." And I realized that connection was to the whole world.

At the monastery, Greg, Phyllis, and Jennifer are constructing the new building and still teaching meditation classes and leading workshops. They have been joined by Cameron, whose anticipated six months has been extended indefinitely. Not long after these interviews, Terry left and Tom returned. Carole has been there for a year now, and others come to stay for varying periods.

❂

ACKNOWLEDGMENTS

My deep gratitude to all the Zen students whose words appear here, not only for sharing their experience, but for their ongoing spiritual practice; to those who helped transcribe tapes and provided photographs; to those who read the manuscript and offered suggestions; and to those who provided housing, transportation, and various forms of sustenance on my visits.

I also wish to thank Mary Sennewald, for valuable editorial advice and invaluable friendship; Murray Suid, for his Zen-like qualities of attention, openness, and compassion; and especially Peter, for his wholehearted support, his kindness and companionship, his library, and his abiding respect for matters of the spirit.

I am grateful for the existence of the Southern Dharma Retreat Center, Hot Springs, North Carolina, where Cheri offers meditation retreats.

Most of all I am grateful for the teacher, and for the teachings.

❂

Cover: Carmel retreat (photograph, Mary Ellen Hammond)

Excerpts are reprinted from the following books:

The Unborn: The Life and Teaching of Zen Master Bankei
Translated by Norman Waddell
North Point Press, 1984

The Diamond Sutra and The Sutra of Hui-neng
Translated by A. F. Price and Wong Mou-Lam
Shambala, 1990

Hakuin's Chant in Praise of Zazen and Seng Tsan's "Affirming
Faith in Mind" in *Zen: Dawn in the West*
Philip Kapleau
Anchor Press/Doubleday, 1980

The Dhammapada
Translated by Eknath Easwaran
Blue Mountain Center of Meditation, 1985

The Lankavatara Scripture and the Surangama Sutra in
A Buddhist Bible
Dwight Goddard
E. P. Dutton and Co., 1966

Zen Master Dogen
Yuho Yokoi
Weatherhill, 1976

Moon in a Dewdrop: Writings of Zen Master Dogen
Edited by Kazuaki Tanahashi
North Point Press, 1985

Yoka-daishi's Song of Realization in *Buddhism and Zen*
Nyogen Senzaki and Ruth Strout McCandless
Philosophical Library, 1953

✿

PUBLICATIONS
FROM A CENTER FOR THE PRACTICE
OF ZEN BUDDHIST MEDITATION

The Key: And the Name of the Key Is Willingness

The How You Do Anything Is How You Do Everything Workbook

That Which You Are Seeking Is Causing You To Seek

The Depression Book

❂